Furt.
Media and Formal Cause

A sage and perceptive quartet of essays which capture and extend a still quintessentially unique way of thinking about media, via patterns and connections that harken to the ancient world and redound to our present and future.

—Paul Levinson, Professor of Communication and Media Studies, Fordham University; author of *Digital McLuhan*, and of *New New Media*

~

This well-chosen collection of essays is essential reading for anyone who wants to think critically about how to understand the pervasive role of media in our world. A provocative and highly innovative perspective on modernity is provided by the use of the notion of formal causation, while new light is also shed on the Aristotelian tradition in which the notion was first developed. This neglected conception of causality remains of profound importance today.

—Paul Franks, Senator Jerahmiel S. and Carole S. Grafstein Chair in Jewish Philosophy, University of Toronto

~

This insightful book entices the reader to engage the legacy of McLuhan. The paradox of formal cause resonates with our post-literate environment. The reader who truly wishes to understand media will recognize the value of these essays.

—Catherine Waite Phelan, Chair and Professor of Communication, Hamilton College; author of *Mediation and the Communication Matrix*

~

Questions about the nature of causality have puzzled philosophers for a very long time. In this collection of papers by and about Marshall McLuhan, we see how these issues can gain new and wider relevance in today's media-focused age. The book illustrates and elucidates McLuhan's thoughts on formal cause, a concept that he believed could help us to grasp the complex relations between media and their effects. In addition to three of McLuhan's own characteristically challenging papers, the associated commentary from Eric McLuhan and Lance Strate help to clarify and contextualize these vital ideas for scholars, artists, and anyone else interested in the fundamental issues of human communication.

—Gerald Erion, Professor of Philosophy, Medaille College

~

Media and Formal Cause

Marshall McLuhan
&
Eric McLuhan

NeoPoiesis Press, LLC

NeoPoiesis Press
P.O. Box 38037
Houston, Texas 77238-8037
www.neopoiesispress.com

Media and Formal Cause by Marshall McLuhan & Eric McLuhan

Includes Bibliography and Index

ISBN 978-0-9832747-0-4 (paperback : alk. paper)
1. Media Studies. 2. Metaphysics. 3. Aesthetics.
I. McLuhan, Marshall II. McLuhan, Eric III. Strate, Lance

Printed in the United States of America
First Edition

Cover Design by Dale Winslow and Quade Zaban
Interior Layout & Design by Erin Badough

Table of Contents

Foreword

Lance Strate

On behalf of NeoPoiesis Press, I would like to express our great pleasure at being able to publish this important little book. It is indeed quite fitting that our first venture outside of the realm of poetry and creative writing is a work that concerns itself with poetics and aesthetics, with the creative process, with *poiesis* both new and old. Moreover, many have commented on the poetic nature of Marshall McLuhan's probes and commentary, and this work, co-authored by Eric McLuhan, is no exception.

Marshall McLuhan (1911-1980) was a professor of English literature long before he became the "media guru" of the western world, and he was the author of a series of highly significant works, including *The Mechanical Bride: Folklore of Industrial Man*,[1] his pioneering study of popular culture and technological society; *The Gutenberg Galaxy*,[2] his scholarly treatise on the transition from speech to writing to print, and beyond, which includes his first major discussion of his notion of the *global village*; *Understanding Media:*

---

[1] Marshall McLuhan, *The Mechanical Bride: Folklore of Industrial Man* (New York: Vanguard Press, 1951).

[2] Marshall McLuhan, *The Gutenberg Galaxy: The Making of Typographic Man* (Toronto: University of Toronto Press, 1962).

The Extensions of Man,[3] one of the most important books of the 20th century, canonical for any field concerned with the study of media, communication, and technology, where McLuhan puts forth his famous maxim that *the medium is the message*; *The Medium is the Massage: An Inventory of Effects*,[4] his bestselling collaboration with artist Quentin Fiore and producer Jerome Agel; *War and Peace in the Global Village*,[5] another work by the McLuhan-Fiore-Agel team; *Through the Vanishing Point: Space in Poetry and Painting*,[6] an exploration of visualism co-authored by Harley Parker; *Counterblast*,[7] another experimental work done in collaboration with Parker; *From Cliché to Archetype*,[8] a return to his literary roots, co-authored by Wilfred Watson; *Take Today: The Executive as Drop Out*,[9] his take on business and organizations in the new electronic environment, co-authored by Barrington Nevitt (McLuhan's co-author for the essay included in Chapter 2 of this volume); and the posthumously published *Laws of Media: The New*

---

3 Marshall McLuhan, *Understanding Media: The Extensions of Man* (New York: McGraw-Hill, 1964).

4 Marshall McLuhan and Quentin Fiore, *The Medium is the Massage: An Inventory of Effects* (New York: Bantam Books, 1967).

5 Marshall McLuhan and Quentin Fiore, *War and Peace in the Global Village: An inventory of some of the current spastic situations that could be eliminated by more feedforward* (New York: Bantam Books, 1968).

6 Marshall McLuhan and Harley Parker, *Through the Vanishing Point: Space in Poetry and Painting* (New York: Harper and Row, 1968).

7 Marshall McLuhan and Harley Parker, *Counterblast* (New York: Harcourt Brace & World, 1969).

8 Marshall McLuhan and Wilfred Watson, *From Cliché to Archetype* (New York: Viking Press, 1970).

9 Marshall McLuhan and Barrington Nevitt, *Take Today: The Executive as Drop Out* (New York: Harcourt Brace Jovanovitch, 1972).

Science, co-authored by Eric McLuhan,[10] his final take on understanding media, for which this book is a crucial supplement (although I hasten to add that *Media and Formal Cause* does not require prior reading of *Laws of Media*). This is far from a complete bibliography of Marshall McLuhan's scholarly production, and books about McLuhan are legion.[11]

Eric McLuhan himself has produced an impressive body of work over the course of his career, and this book holds special significance for me because it was the better part of a decade ago, when I was editing the Media Ecology Association's new journal, *Explorations in Media Ecology*, that Eric McLuhan sent me his extended essay, entitled "On Formal Cause." Aside from the fact that it was twice as long as the standard journal article, I must confess that I was not sure what to make of it initially. This was the first I had heard of *formal cause*, and I found it rather difficult to understand at first, although I could sense that this article represented a major breakthrough for McLuhan studies, and therefore for media ecology. Looking back on it now, I imagine that I must have been in somewhat the same position as Neil Postman was at the time that Neil was editing the journal *ETC: A Review of General Semantics*, and received as a submission Marshall McLuhan's "Laws of Media" article.[12] Neil turned to one of his doctoral students who was assisting him on *ETC*, Paul Levinson, for his assessment of the article. Paul was

---

[10] Marshall McLuhan and Eric McLuhan, *Laws of Media: The New Science* (Toronto: University of Toronto Press, 1988).

[11] Including my own contributions: Lance Strate and Edward Wachtel, eds., *The Legacy of McLuhan* (Cresskill, NJ: Hampton Press, 2005), and Lance Strate, *Echoes and Reflections: On Media Ecology as a Field of Study* (Cresskill, NJ: Hampton Press, 2006).

[12] Marshall McLuhan, "Laws of Media," *ETC: A Review of General Semantics* 34:2 (1977): 173-179.

extremely enthusiastic upon reading it, and ended up writing an introduction to the article to emphasize its importance. Coincidentally, Paul Levinson was my colleague at Fordham University, and without realizing it, I repeated the pattern by asking him to read Eric's piece, and then moving forward based on Paul's strong recommendations. I suppose you could say that this pattern that connects is the formal cause of this book you now hold in your hands.

After a bit of editorial work on my part, and then some significant labor on the part the publisher of *Explorations in Media Ecology* at that time, Hampton Press, in regard to the copyediting and layout of a piece that in a number of ways diverged from the typical journal article, "On Formal Cause" was published in *Explorations in Media Ecology* Volume 4, Numbers 3/4 (a double issue due in large part to the length of the essay), in 2005.[13] Of course, by that time, I had come to understand the concept of formal causality, and its significance. And I began to recognize it as it popped up in many different places, typically without being identified as such. For example, consider the following passage from Martin Buber's classic work, *I and Thou*:

> This is the eternal source of art: a man is faced by a form which desires to be made through him into a work. This form is no offspring of his soul, but is an appearance which steps up to it and demands of it the effective power. The man is concerned with an act of his being. If he carries it through, if he speaks the primary word out of his being to the

[13] Eric McLuhan, "On Formal Cause," *Explorations in Media Ecology* 4:3/4 (2005): 181-210.

> form which appears, then the effective power streams out, and the work arises.[14]

Indeed, as Buber indicates, there is a spiritual dimension to formal causality, as there is to all acts of creation. But for those who prefer a more scientific outlook, let me simply note that formal cause corresponds to the systems view of Gregory Bateson,[15] to the dissipative structures of physicist Ilya Prigogine[16], to the fractal geometry of Benoit Mandelbrot[17] and the metapatterns of Tyler Volk,[18] to the autopoietic systems of biologists Humberto Maturana and Francisco Varela,[19] and in general to the systems concept of emergence[20].

McLuhan, along with other media ecology scholars, has been accused of being a technological determinist. And while technological determinism has largely been used as a straw man argument to dismiss McLuhan and others without due consideration, the deterministic language of cause-and-effect is easy enough to slip into, by force of habit, and for wont of easily accessible alternatives. Thus, we may end up

---

14 Martin Buber, *I and Thou*, Ronald Gregor Smith, Trans. (New York: Macmillan, 1958): 9-10.

15 Gregory Bateson, *Steps to an Ecology of Mind: Collected Essays in Anthropology, Psychiatry, Evolution, and Epistemology* (Chicago: University Of Chicago Press, 1972).

16 Ilya Prigogine and Isabelle Stengers, *Order Out of Chaos: Man's New Dialogue with Nature* (London: Flamingo, 1984).

17 Benoit Mandelbrot, *The Fractal Geometry of Nature* (San Francisco, CA: W. H. Freeman, 1983).

18 Tyler Volk, *Metapatterns Across Space, Time, and Mind* (New York: Columbia University Press, 1995).

19 Humberto R. Maturana and Francisco J. Varela, *Autopoiesis and Cognition: The Realization of the Living* (Boston : D. Reidel, 1980).

20 For a popular introduction, see Steven Johnson, *Emergence: The Connected Lives of Ants, Brains, Cities, and Software* (New York: Scribner, 2001).

with statements like, *the stirrup caused feudalism* as a shorthand, in the same way that we might say that evolution *caused* us to walk erect. For media ecologists and biologists alike, we understand that that kind of language is a form of shorthand, and a kind of poetry, used to represent much more complex processes. That complexity can be better represented by the concept of formal cause, rather than cause-and-effect (otherwise known as efficient cause); formal cause is the causality of emergent properties, the causality that media ecologists often have in mind when we consider the impact of technological change on individuals and societies, on communication, consciousness, and culture. It is also interesting to note that formal cause is a radical departure from formal logic, that Aristotle's metaphysics is a far cry from his dialectics and rhetorics. In this sense, Eric McLuhan presents us with a decidedly non-Aristotelian (in the Korzybskian sense) Aristotle, an Aristotle that is consistent with general semantics.[21]

When "On Formal Cause" was originally published, there was a footnote that read:

> I earnestly hope the reader will also look up three essays by Marshall McLuhan in which he discusses formal cause in relation to matters he studied. The first is the essay, "The Relation of Environment to Anti-Environment," in *University of Windsor Review*, Vol. 11, No. 1, Fall, 1966, (Windsor, Ontario), pp. 1-10. Rpt., Floyd Matson and Ashley Montagu, eds., *The Human Dialogue* (New York: Macmillan, 1967), pp. 1-10. The second, "*The Argument: Causality*

[21] Alfred Korzybski, *Science and Sanity: An Introduction to Non-Aristotelian Systems and General Semantics*, 5th ed. (Englewood, NJ: Institute of General Semantics, 1994).

in the Electric World," by Marshall McLuhan and Barrington Nevitt, appeared in *Technology and Culture*, Vol. 14, #1 (University of Chicago Press, January, 1973), pp. 1-18. The responses by Fr. Joseph Owens (pp. 19-21) and Dr. Fritz Wilhelmsen, pp. (22-27) also merit attention. The third, "Formal Causality in Chesterton," appeared in *The Chesterton Review*, Spring / Summer, 1976, Vol. II, No. 2, pp. 253-259.[22]

As you can see, the form of this book was present well before the publication of Eric McLuhan's essay, let alone the publication of this book. That particular footnote has been removed as unnecessary, now that we have brought together the three essays Eric recommended, followed by his extended essay, with an original introduction that he has provided for this volume. I would note as well that some modest revisions have been made to the four chapters, mostly in regard to citations and footnotes, and some material has been restored to "On Formal Cause" that was cut in the original publication, including, on my request, Eric's humorous *preamble*. As you, the reader, are also the formal cause of this book, on behalf of NeoPoiesis Press I thank you for making *Media and Formal Cause* possible.

---

[22] Op. Cit.: 204.

Introduction

To the Western mind, the most mysterious feature of formal cause is its paradoxical relation to effects. The familiar ritual of cause-and-effect[23] occurs in a sequence but is quite unable to explain the nature of media. Formal cause is in many ways synonymous with medium but it is riddled with paradox. By 1964, Marshall McLuhan had identified media themselves as the cause of change in psyche and society alike, and he had discovered that media exert environmental pressures. He developed this idea at some length in "The Relation of Environment to Anti-environment." *Understanding Media* provides this probe in the first chapter:

> The railway did not introduce movement or transportation or wheel or road into human society, but it accelerated and enlarged the scale of previous human functions, creating totally new kinds of cities and new kinds of work and leisure. This happened whether the railway functioned in a tropical or a northern environment, and is quite independent of the freight or content of the railway medium.[24]

---

[23] Often called "the causal principle."

[24] Marshall McLuhan, *Understanding Media: The Extensions of Man* (New York: McGraw Hill, 1964): 8.

The medium of the railroad, and that of every other human technology, is the environment of services and disservices that the railroad brings into play. "Any extension," he wrote, "whether of skin, hand, or foot, affects the whole psychic and social complex."[25] There was, and is, nothing in the normal ways of unfolding causality, that permits us to examine environments as causes.

> It is in the interplay between the old and the new environments that there is generated an innumerable series of problems and confusions. They extend all the way from how to allocate the time of children and adults to the problem of pay-TV and TV in the classroom. The new medium of TV as an environment creates new occupations. As an environment, it is imperceptible except in terms of its content. That is, all that is seen or noticed is the old environment, the movie. But the effects of TV on the movie go unnoticed, and the effects of the TV environment in altering the entire character of human sensibility and sensory ratios is completely ignored.[26]

In the literate world, the function of liberal studies, of all the arts and sciences, had been at least in part to serve as counter-environments, as a means of orientation and perception. The situations is somewhat different in our post-literate condition:

> In a preliterate society art serves as a means of merging the individual and the environment, not as a means of training perception upon the environment. Archaic or primitive art looks to

---

25 Ibid.: 4.

26 See chapter 1 of this volume, p.

> us like a magical control built into the environment.
>
> Thus to put the artefacts from such a culture into a museum or anti-environment is an act of nullification rather than of revelation. Today what is called "Pop Art" is the use of some object in our own daily environment as if it were anti-environmental. Pop Art serves to remind us, however, that we have fashioned for ourselves a world of artefacts and images that are intended not to train perception or awareness but to insist that we merge with them as the primitive man merges with his environment.[27]

While not formally "about" formal cause, this essay is effectively an anatomy of it and anticipates the discussions that follow. Our practice of using art as therapy for the mentally disturbed reminds us that we are today deep in the primitive condition.

But while he knew the route to understanding media new or old was to be traced in the actions of environments and not of their contents or uses, the matter of an appropriate causality still eluded him. In 1969, he wrote to Jacques Maritain,

> I am quite aware that nobody has attempted to understand metamorphosis and causality in social institutions through a minute inspection of the sensory and perceptual changes resulting from the new environments. Surely the history of philosophy can never be written without a complete awareness of these matters.[28]

---

[27] Ibid.

[28] Letter dated May 28, 1969. Unpublished. Maritain, along with Etienne Gilson, had for some time been working and teaching at

Maritain responded by urging that he pay more attention to formal cause:

> I am in overall agreement with what you have written to me... This, in its way, plays an essential role, which you insist on with good reason. But it does not account for everything. For, there is also formal causality, and I fear that you have not taken sufficient account of its role.[29]

Of all of his colleagues and correspondents at this time, Jacques Maritain appears to have been the only one to point him in the direction of formal cause as relating to media. Over the next years we consulted every source we could find in pursuit of a useable explanation of formal cause, with little result.

Still in pursuit of environmental causality, in 1971, McLuhan wrote to Ashley Montagu about this matter:

> In recent years I've been working on causation. More and more I feel compelled to consider causation as following from effects. That is, the effects of the telegraph created an environment of information that made the telephone a perfectly natural development. In a certain sense, therefore, the effects of the telephone provided the invention of the actual hardware instrument. This, of course, is non-lineal, non-sequential causality. In fact, it suggests that

---

the Pontifical Institute for Medieval Studies, a few yards distance from McLuhan's office on the campus of St. Michael's College. Collegial conversations were not infrequent.

29 Letter written from Kolbsheim, dated 10 August, 1969. Unpublished.

> causes and effects are simultaneous, if anything.[30]

Clearly the other three forms of causality in Aristotle's system did not answer the question, how do media/environments (such as print or television or radio) exert their powers on the users? Final cause is of no use. The final cause of, say, a house is the house; of a car, the car; of a radio, the radio set; and so on. The material cause is simply the matter of which the item is composed. And the efficient cause is the process of making the object and the maker himself. That left the formal cause, which had for many centuries been the subject of debate. No-one was really certain as to what exactly it was—a condition that still obtains. Or rather, various groups of philosophers were more or less certain, but they did not agree. Nor was Aristotle himself a great deal of help, as he seemed to vacillate in his thoughts about the matter from one text to another.

Take the example of a car. The *material cause* would be the iron and steel and plastic, the wiring and fabrics and other components of which the artifact, the car, is composed. The *efficient cause* includes the makers and the making process, the assembly line and so on. The *final cause* would be the car itself, the *ding an sich*, the thing minus its *ground*. The *formal cause* is traditionally regarded as being the blueprint or design of the car—the form given to the matter by the maker. And these interpretations fit nicely with the familiar categories of matter and form. But they do not quite fit Aristotle's explanations. Maritain suspected that formal cause was quirky enough to

---

[30] Letter dated October 22, 1971. From *Letters of Marshall McLuhan*, eds. Matie Molinaro, Corrine McLuhan, and William Toye (Toronto: Oxford University Press, 1987) 446.

approximate my father's notions about the ways media of communication worked on cultures.

In 1971, he wrote to Jim Davey at the Prime Minister's Office,

> Only yesterday I was reading a chapter on "Judgment and Truth in Aquinas" by my friend, Fr. Owens, here at the Medieval Institute. He concludes: "They involve the traditional Aristotelian view that the cognitive agent is and becomes the thing known. . . . Its structure comes from the thing known, and not from any apriori in the intellect." [31]
>
> It turns out then, that my communication theory is Thomistic to the core. It has the further advantage of being able to explain Aquinas and Aristotle in modern terms. We are the content of anything we use, if only because these things are extensions of ourselves. The meaning of the pencil, or the chair I use is the interplay between me and these things. Again, the message of these things is the sum of the changes that result from their social use. Thus, I have added two features to "the medium is the message", namely the content and the meaning.[32]

At the time of writing these lines, the book with Barry Nevitt was nearing completion: *Take Today: the Executive as Dropout,* a discussion of management practices.[33] A few months later, "Causality in the Electric World," by McLuhan and Nevitt, appeared in

---

31 *Medieval Studies* 33 (1970): 138-158.

32 *Letters*, Letter of March 8, 1971, p. 427.

33 Marshall McLuhan and Barrington Nevitt, *Take Today: the Executive as Dropout* (New York: Harcourt Brace Jovanovich, 1972).

Technology and Culture,[34] which printed this article together with responses by Fr. Joseph Owens[35] and Dr. Frederick Wilhelmsen. The editor attempted to establish a 3-way conversation between the main article and these two medieval philosophers, one at the University of Toronto and one at the University of Dallas. The interactions, and the misunderstandings, between the article and their responses reveal a great deal about how things happen in this world, and how we imagine the world to be. Each respondent misses Mcluhan's/Nevitt's central point in his own way. Formal causality, in which coming events cast their shadows (effects) before them, is hugely mysterious: the literate mind simply can't grasp it; it is too paradoxical. It deals with environmental processes, which are not sequential and which therefore baffle any rational attempt to come to grips with it. Dr. Wilhelmsen has an advantage in that he is a fan of G. K. Chesterton's writing: Chesterton reveled in the type of thinking that could play with contradictory or paradoxical structures and situations. "Causality in the Electric World" presents an important statement of philosophical as well as practical import concerning the nature of causality in an all-at-once world. The electric world is quite different from the familiar 18th and 19th century worlds in which events happened one-thing-at-a-time.

Not long after beginning to discuss how media change perception and transform cultures, McLuhan began also to encounter strong resistance to his expositions. He was describing a kind of causation that people, particularly those trained in the sciences, simply did not want to admit existed. It was irrational.

---

[34] *Technology and Culture* 14:1 (1973): 1-18. Fr. Owens's response followed on pp.19-21, and Dr. Wilhelmsen's on pp. 22-27.

[35] Then at the Pontifical Institute for Medieval Studies.

This made him the more curious about the varieties of causality and the kinds of blindness they inspired. In some exasperation, he remarked, a couple of years before writing "Causality in the Electric World" that

> People do not want to know the cause of anything. They do not want to know why radio caused Hitler and Ghandi alike. They do not want to know that print caused anything whatever. As users of these media, they wish merely to get inside, hoping perhaps to add another layer to their environment in the manner of "The Chambered Nautilus" of Oliver Wendell Holmes.
>
> The total non-response of hundreds of thousands of people to the suggestion that there was an actual physical environmental, man-made cause of drug addiction in our time startled me into study of the attitude of the scientific community to causation. It does not take long to discover that all of the sciences, physical and social, are interested only in describing and measuring effects while ignoring causation entirely. A *connection* is not a cause but a hang-up... the absence of interest in causation cannot persist in the new age of ecology. Ecology does not seek connections, but patterns. It does not seek quantities, but satisfactions and understanding. The pioneer work of Harold Innis in the study of causality relating to the material media of communication had no followers, despite his being surrounded with academic admirers. The student of media will discover that for the past 500 years Western Science has systematically

> excluded the study of causation by the simple process of fragmentation and quantification.[36]

In the next few years, McLuhan never ceased to examine the structural characteristics of the kinds of causality that media exercise on perception and culture. "Causality in the Electric World" is one result of that preoccupation. Perhaps its signal contribution to our theme was the discovery that formal cause coincided with ground—situation or environment.

If you know Dr. McLuhan's usual writing style, you may be surprised at the style here, at the sometimes impish, prankish and playful voice. The differences owe much to the contributions of the co-author, Mr. Nevitt.

Not long after the publication of "Causality in the Electric World," McLuhan wrote the little piece (included here as chapter three) on Chesterton, his only essay on an individual artist's use of formal causality, and also his last statement in print on the business. In a letter to his old friend, Archie Malloch, he wrote,

> Casuistry seems to be the second part of rhetoric, i.e., *dispositio* or *method.* The Puritans latched on to it as a way of getting rid of the four levels and it also had the effect of abolishing the doctrine of decorum and the levels of style. *Dispositio* is, above all, visual and applied knowledge and is inseparable from dialectic, whether in Aquinas or in Hegel. One big discovery I have made a propos Aquinas is that every article of his uses the five divisions of rhetoric. His *objections* represent the *formal* causality of his endeavours, namely, his public.

---

[36] See Chap. 4, note 95.

> My discovery that formal causality is always the audience dawned on me while reading an essay by Arthur Miller on the disappearance of his public: "1949: The Year It Came Apart" (*New York* magazine, January, 1975). Communication theory necessarily concerns the study of the public and not of the program. The "content" of any performance is the efficient cause which includes the user or the cognitive agent who is, and becomes, the thing known, in Aristotle's phrase.[37]

My own contribution to this collection, "On Formal Cause," was provoked by a succession of inane remarks on the Internet about the nature of formal cause and its relation to media. The writers had thoroughly scrambled matters, and confused the other readers. In writing, I enjoyed the advantage of thirty years' distance from our earlier investigations, and I had learned a little in the interim, including some Greek. I returned to the source, Aristotle, and discovered that he was of two minds about formal cause. He did identify formal cause with *logos*, but that word had in his time acquired two somewhat different meanings and he never sorted them out for us. I also had the benefit of Eric Havelock's wonderful studies, *Preface to Plato*,[38] and *Prologue to Greek Literacy*,[39] and many conversations with learned colleagues, to mention a few. How could one go wrong with such guides?

Eric McLuhan, Bloomfield, 2010.

---

[37] Dated January 5, 1976. Unpublished.
[38] Eric Havelock, *Preface to Plato* (Cambridge, MA: The Belknap Press of Harvard University Press, 1963).
[39] Eric Havelock, *Prologue to Greek Literacy* (Cincinnati: University of Cincinnati, 1971).

Chapter One

The Relation of Environment to Anti-Environment

Marshall McLuhan

Under the heading that "What exists is likely to be misallocated" Peter Drucker in *Managing for Results*[40] discusses the structure of social situations. "Business enterprise is not a phenomenon of nature but one of society. In a social situation, however, events are not distributed according to the "normal distribution" of a natural universe (that is, they are not distributed according to the bell-shaped Gaussian curve). In a social situation a very small number of events at one extreme—the first 10 per cent to 20 per cent at most—account for 90 per cent of all results; whereas the great majority of events accounts for 10 per cent or so of all the results." What Drucker is presenting here is the environment as it presents itself for human attention and action. He is confronting the phenomenon of the imperceptibility of

[40] Peter F. Drucker, *Managing for Results: Economic Tasks and Risk-Taking Decisions.* (New York: Harper & Row, 1964).

the environment as such. It is this factor that Edward T. Hall also tackles in *The Silent Language*.[41] The ground rules, the pervasive structure, the overall pattern eludes perception except in so far as there is an Anti-Environment or a counter-situation constructed to provide a means of direct attention. Paradoxically, the 10 per cent of the typical situation that Drucker designates as the area of effective cause and as the area of opportunity, this small factor is the environment. The 90 per cent area is the area of problems generated by the active power of the 10 per cent environment. For the environment is an active process pervading and impinging upon all the components of the situation. It is easy to illustrate this.

Any new technology, any extension or amplification of human faculties when given material embodiment, tends to create a new environment. This is as true of clothing as of speech, or script, or wheel. This process is more easily observed in our own time when several new environments have been created. To take only the latest one, TV, we find a handful of engineers and technicians in the 10 per cent area, as it were, creating a set of radical changes in the 90 per cent area of daily life. The new TV environment is an electric circuit that takes as its content the earlier environment, the photograph and the movie in particular. It is in the interplay between the old and the new environments that there is generated an innumerable series of problems and confusions. They extend all the way from how to allocate the time of children and adults to the problem of pay-TV and TV in the classroom. The new medium of TV as an environment creates new occupations. As an

---

[41] Edward T. Hall, *The Silent Language* (Garden City, NY: Doubleday, 1959).

environment, it is imperceptible except in terms of its content. That is, all that is seen or noticed is the old environment, the movie. But the effects of TV on the movie go unnoticed, and the effects of the TV environment in altering the entire character of human sensibility and sensory ratios is completely ignored.

The content of any system or organization naturally consists of the preceding system or organization, and in that degree acts as a control on the new environment. It is useful to notice all of the arts and sciences as acting in the role of Anti-Environments that enable us to perceive the environment. In a business civilization we have long considered liberal study as providing necessary means of orientation and perception. When the arts and sciences themselves become environments under conditions of electric circuitry, conventional liberal studies whether in the arts or sciences will no longer serve as an Anti-Environment. When we live in a museum without walls, or have music as a structural part of our sensory environment, new strategies of attention and perception have to be created. When the highest scientific knowledge creates the environment of the atom bomb, new controls for the scientific environment have to be discovered, if only in the interest of survival.

The structural examples of the relation of environment to Anti-Environment need to be multiplied as a means of understanding the principles of perception and activity involved. The Balinese say: "We have no art—we do everything as well as possible." This is not an ironic but a merely factual remark. In a preliterate society art serves as a means of merging the individual and the environment, not as a means of training perception upon the environment. Archaic or primitive art looks to us like a magical control built into the environment. Thus to put the artefacts from such a culture into a museum or Anti-Environment is an act of nullification rather than of revelation. Today what is called "Pop Art" is the use of some object in our own daily environment as if it were Anti-Environmental. Pop Art serves to remind us, however, that we have fashioned for ourselves a world of artefacts and images that are intended not to train perception or awareness but to insist that we merge with them as the primitive man merges with his environment. The world of modern advertising is a magical environment constructed to produce effects for the total economy but not designed to increase human awareness. We have designed schools as Anti-Environments to develop the perception and judgment of the printed word. There are no means of training provided to develop similar perceptions and judgment of any of the new environments created by electric circuitry. This is not accidental. From the development of phonetic script until the invention of the electric telegraph human technology had tended strongly towards the furtherance of detachment and objectivity, detribalization and individuality. Electric circuitry has quite the contrary effect. It involves in depth. It merges the individual and the mass environment. To create an Anti-Environment for such electric technology would seem to require a technological extension of consciousness itself. The awareness and opposition of the individual are in these circumstances as irrelevant as they are futile.

The structural features of environment and Anti-Environment appear in the age-old clash between professionalism and amateurism, whether in sport or in studies. Professional sport is environmental and amateur sport is Anti-Environmental. Professional sport fosters the merging of the individual in the mass and in the patterns of the total environment. Amateur sport seeks rather the development of critical awareness of the individual and most of all, critical awareness of the ground rules of the society as such. The same contrast exists for studies. The professional tends to specialize and to merge his being uncritically in the mass. The ground rules provided by the mass response of his colleagues serve as a pervasive environment of which he is uncritical and unaware.

The party system of government affords a familiar image of the relations of environment and Anti-Environment. The government as environment needs the opposition as Anti-Environment in order to be aware of itself. The role of the opposition would seem to be that of the arts and sciences in creating perception. As the government environment becomes more cohesively involved in a world of instant information, opposition would seem to become increasingly necessary but also intolerable. Opposition begins to assume the rancorous and hostile character of a Dew Line, or a Distant Early Warning System. It is important, however, to consider the role of the arts and sciences as Early Warning Systems in the social environment. The models of perception provided in the arts and sciences alike can serve as indispensable means of orientation to future problems well before they become troublesome.

The legend of Humpty-Dumpty would seem to suggest a parallel to the 10%-90% distribution of causes and effects. The impact that resulted in his fall brought into play a massive response from the social bureaucracy. But all the King's horses and all the King's men could not put Humpty-Dumpty back together again. They could not recreate the old environment, they could only create a new one. Our typical response to a disrupting new technology is to recreate the old environment instead of heeding the new opportunities of the new environment. Failure to notice the new opportunities is also failure to understand the new powers. This means that we fail to develop the necessary controls or Anti-Environments for the new environment. The failure leaves us in the role of automata merely.

W. T. Easterbrook[42] has done extensive exploration of the relations of bureaucracy and enterprise, discovering that as soon as one becomes the environment, the other becomes an Anti-Environment. They seem to bicycle along through history alternating their roles with all the dash and vigor of tweedle-dum and tweedle-dee. In the 18th century when *realism* became a new method in literature, what happened was that the external environment was put in the place of Anti-Environment. The ordinary world was given the role of art object by Daniel Defoe and others. The environment began to be used as a perceptual probe. It became self-conscious. It became an "anxious object" instead of being an unperceived and pervasive pattern. Environment used as probe or art object is satirical because it draws attention to itself. The romantic poets extended this technique to external nature transforming nature into an art object. Beginning with Baudelaire and Rimbaud and continuing in Hopkins and Eliot and James Joyce, the poets turned their attention to language as a probe. Long used as an environment, language became an instrument of exploration and research. It became an Anti-Environment. It became Pop Art.

The artist as a maker of Anti-Environments permits us to perceive that much is newly environmental and therefore most active in transforming situations. This would seem to be why the artist has in many circles in the past century been

---

[42] See, for example, W. T. Easterbrook and Hugh G. J. Aitken, *Canadian Economic History* (Toronto: Macmillan, 1956).

called the enemy, the criminal. It helps to explain why news has a natural bias toward crime and bad news. It is this kind of news that enables us to perceive our world. The detective since Poe's Dupin has tended to be a probe, an artist of the big town, an artist-enemy, as it were. Conventionally, society is always one phase back, is never environmental. Paradoxically, it is the antecedent environment that is always being upgraded for our attention. The new environment always uses the old environment as its material.

In the Spring issue of the *Varsity Grad* (1965) Glenn Gould discusses the effects of recorded music on performance and composition.[43] One of his main points is that as recorded music creates a new environment the audience in effect becomes participant both in performance and in composition. This is a reversal or chiasmus of form that occurs in any situation where an environment is pushed up into high intensity or high definition by technological change. A reversal of characteristics occurs as in the case with bureaucracy and enterprise. An environment is naturally of low intensity or low definition. That is why it escapes observation. Anything that raises the environment to high intensity, whether it be a storm in nature or violent change resulting from a new technology, such high intensity turns the environment into an object of attention. When an environment becomes an object of attention it assumes the character of Anti-Environment or an art object. When the social environment is stirred up to exceptional intensity by technological change and becomes the focus of much attention, we apply the terms "war" and "revolution." All the components of "war" are present in any

[43] Glenn Gould, "An Argument for Music in the Electronic Age," *Varsity Graduate* 11:3 (1964): 118-120.

environment whatever. The recognition of war depends upon their being stepped up to high definition.

Under electric conditions of instant information movement both the concept and the reality of war become manifest in many of the situations of daily life. We have long been accustomed to war as that which goes on between publics or nations. Publics and nations were the creation of print technology. With electric circuitry the publics and nations become the content of the new technology: "The mass audience is not a public as environment but a public as content of a new electric environment." And whereas "the public" as an environment created by print technology consisted of separate individuals with varying points of view, the mass audience consists of the same individuals involved in depth in one another and involved in the creative process of the art or educational situation that is presented to them. Art and education were presented to the *public* as consumer packages for their instruction and edification. The new mass audience is involved immediately in art and education as participants and co-creators rather than as consumers. Art and education become new forms of experience, new environments, rather than new Anti-Environments. Pre-electric art and education were Anti-Environments in the sense that they were the content of various environments. Under electric conditions the content tends however towards becoming environmental itself. This was the paradox that Malraux found in *The Museum Without Walls*,[44] and that Glenn Gould finds in recorded music. Music in the concert hall had been an Anti-Environment. The same music when recorded is *music without halls*, as it were.

---

44 André Malraux, *The Museum Without Walls*, trans. Stuart Gilbert (London : A. Zwemmer, 1949).

Another paradoxical aspect of this change is that when music becomes environmental by electric means, it becomes more and more the concern of the private individual. By the same token and complementary to the same paradox the pre-electric music of the concert hall (the music when there was a public instead of a mass audience) was a corporate ritual for the group rather than the individual. This paradox extends to all electrical technology whatever. The same means which permit, for example, a universal and centralized thermostat do in effect encourage a private thermostat for individual manipulation. The age of the mass audience is thus far more individualistic than the preceding age of the *public*. It is this paradoxical dynamic that confuses every issue about "conformity" today and "separatism" and "integration." Profoundly contradictory actions and directions prevail in all of these situations. This is not surprising in an age of circuitry succeeding the age of the wheel. The feedback loop plays all sorts of tricks to confound the single plane and one-way direction of thought and action as they had been constituted in the pre-electric age of the machine.

Applying the above to the Negro question, one could say that the agrarian South has long tended to regard the Negro as environmental. As such, the Negro is a challenge, a threat, a burden. The very phrase "white supremacy" quite as much as the phrase "white trash" registers this environmental attitude. The environment is the enemy that must be subdued. To the rural man the conquest of Nature is an unceasing challenge. It is the Southerner who contributed the cowboy to the frontier. The Virginian, the archetypal cowboy as it were, confronts the environment as a hostile, natural force. To man on the frontier, other men are environmental and hostile. By contrast, to the townsman, men appear not as environmental, but as content of the urban environment.

Parallel to the Negro question is the French Canada problem. The English Canadians have been the environment of French Canada since the railway and Confederation. However, since the telegraph and radio and television, French Canada and English Canada alike have become the content of this new technology. Electric technology is totally environmental for all human communities today. Hence the great confusion arising from the transformation of environments into Anti-Environments, as it were. All the earlier groupings that had constituted separate environments before electricity have now become Anti-Environments or the content of the new technology. As such, the old unconscious environments tend to become increasingly centres of acute awareness. The content of any new environment is just as unperceived as the old one had been initially. As a merely automatic sequence, the succession of environments and of the dramatics thereto appertaining, tend to be rather tiresome, if only because the audience is very prone to participate in the dramatics with an enthusiasm proportional to its unawareness. In the electric age all former environments whatever become Anti-Environments. As such, the old environments are transformed into areas of self-awareness and self-assertion, guaranteeing a very lively interplay of forces.

Eric Havelock in his book *Preface to Plato*[45] has clarified the stages by which the written word served to detribalize the Greek world. After the tribal encyclopedia of oral and memorized wisdom, writing enabled man to organize knowledge by categories and

---

45 Havelock, *Preface,* op. cit.

classifications; what Plato called the *ideas*. With the origin of classified data, or visual organization of knowledge, there came also representation in the arts. Representation is itself a form of matching or classifying, unknown to preliterate or native artists. Today we return to non-objective art, non-representational art, because in the electric age we are leaving the world of visual organization of experience.

The visual sense, alone of our senses, creates the forms of space and time that are uniform, continuous and connected. Euclidean space is the prerogative of visual and literate man. With the advent of electric circuitry and the instant movement of information, Euclidean space recedes and the non-Euclidean geometries emerge. Lewis Carroll, the Oxford mathematician, was perfectly aware of this change in our world when he took Alice through the looking-glass into the world where each object creates its own space and conditions. To the visual or Euclidean man, objects do not create time and space. They are merely fitted into time and space. The idea of the world as an environment that is more or less fixed, is very much the product of literacy and visual assumptions. In his book, *The Philosophical Impact of Contemporary Physics* Milic Capek[46] explains some of the strange confusions in the scientific mind that result from the encounter of the old non-Euclidean spaces of preliterate man with the Euclidean and Newtonian spaces of literate man. The scientists of our time are just as confused as the philosophers, or the teachers, and it is for the reason that Whitehead assigned; they still have the illusion that the new developments are to be fitted into the old space or environment.

---

[46] Milic Capek, *The Philosophical Impact of Contemporary Physics* (New York: Van Nostrand, 1961).

One of the most obvious areas of change in the arts of our time has not only been the dropping of representation, but the dropping of the story line. In poetry, in the novel, in the movie, narrative continuity has yielded to thematic variation. Such variation in place of story line or melodic line has always been the norm in native societies. It is now becoming the norm in our society and for the same reason, namely that we are becoming a non-visual society.

In the age of circuitry, or feedback, fragmentation and specialism tend to yield to integral forms of organization. Humpty-Dumpty tends to go back together again. The bureaucratic efforts of all the King's horses and all the King's men were naturally calculated to keep Humpty-Dumpty from ever getting together again. The Neolithic age, the age of the planter after the age of the hunter, was an age of specialism and division of labour. It has reached a somewhat startling terminus with the advent of electric circuitry, Circuitry is a profoundly decentralizing process. Paradoxically, it was the wheel and mechanical innovation that created centralism. The circuit reverses the characteristics of the wheel, just as Xerography reverses the characteristics of the printing press. Before printing, the scribe, the author, and the reader tended to merge. With printing, author and publisher became highly specialized and centralized forms of action. With Xerography, author, and publisher, and reader tend to merge once more. Whereas the printed book had been the first mass-produced product, creating uniform prices and markets, Xerography tends to restore the custom-made book. Writing and publishing tend to become services of a corporate and inclusive kind. The printed word created the Public. The Public consists of separate individuals, each with his own point of view. Electric circuitry does not create a Public. It creates the Mass. The Mass does not consist of separate individuals, but of individuals profoundly involved in one another, This involvement is a function, not of numbers, but of speed. The daily newspaper is an interesting example of this fact. The items in the daily press are totally discontinuous and totally unconnected. The only unifying feature of the press is the date line. Through that date line the reader must go, as Alice went, 'through the looking glass.' If it is not today's date line, he cannot get in. Once he goes through the date line, he is involved in a world of items for which he, the reader, must write a story line. He makes the news, as the reader of a detective story makes the plot.

Just as the printed press crated the Public as a new environment, so does each new technology or extension of our physical powers tend to create new environments. In the age of information, it is information itself that becomes environmental. The satellites and antennae projected from our planet, for example, have transformed the planet from being an environment into being a probe. This is a transformation which the artists of the past century have been explaining to us in their endless experimental models. Modern art, whether in painting, or poetry, or music, began as a probe and not as a package. The Symbolists literally broke up the old packages and put them into our hands as probes. And whereas the package belongs to the consumer age, the probe belongs to an age of experimenters.

One of the peculiarities of art is to serve as Anti-Environment, a probe that makes the environment visible. It is a form of symbolic, or parabolic, action. Parable means literally "to throw against," just as symbol means "to throw together." As we equip the planet with satellites and antennae, we tend to create new environments of which the planet itself is the content. It is peculiar to environments that they are complex processes which transform their content into archetypal forms. As the planet becomes the content of a new information environment, it also tends to become a work of art. Where railway and machine created a new environment for agrarian man, the old agrarian world became an art form. Nature became a work of art. The Romantic movement was born. When the electric circuit went around the mechanical environment, the machine itself became a work of art. Abstract art was born.

As information becomes our environment, it becomes mandatory to program the environment itself as a work of art. The parallel to this appears in Jacques Ellul's *Propaganda*[47] where he sees propaganda, not as an ideology or content of any medium, but as the operation of all the media at once. The mother tongue is propaganda because it exercises an effect on all the senses at once. It shapes our entire outlook and our ways of feeling, Like any other environment, its operation is imperceptible. When an environment is new, we perceive the old one for the first time. What we see on the late show is not TV, but old movies. When the Emperor appeared in his new clothes, his courtiers did not see his nudity, they saw his old clothes. Only the small child and the artist have that immediacy of approach that permits perception of the environmental. The artist provides us with Anti-Environments that enable us to see the environment. Such Anti-Environmental means of perception must constantly be renewed in order to be efficacious. That basic aspect of the human condition by which we are rendered incapable of perceiving the environment is one to which psychologists have not

---

[47] Jacques Ellul, *Propaganda: The Formation of Men's Attitudes*, trans. Konrad Kellen and Jean Lerner (New York: Knopf, 1965).

even referred. In an age of accelerated change, the need to perceive the environment becomes urgent. Acceleration also makes such perception of the environment more possible. Was it not Bertrand Russell who said that if the bath water got only half a degree warmer every hour, we would never know when to scream? New environments reset our sensory thresholds. These in turn, alter our outlook and expectations.

The need of our time is for the means of measuring sensory thresholds and of discovering exactly what changes occur in these thresholds as a result of the advent of any particular technology. With such knowledge in hand, it would be possible to program a reasonable and orderly future for any human community. Such knowledge would be the equivalent of a thermostatic control for room temperatures. It would seem only reasonable to extend such controls to all the sensory thresholds of our being. We have no reason to be grateful to those who juggle the thresholds in the name of haphazard innovation.

Chapter Two

Causality in the Electric World

Marshall McLuhan and Barrington Nevitt[48] with responses by Joseph Owens and Frederick D. Willhelmsen

[48] In the original publication in *Technology and Culture,* the following author identifications appeared: DR. MCLUHAN, Director of the Centre for Culture and Technology at the University of Toronto, is the author of *The Gutenberg Galaxy, Understanding Media,* and other books and articles heralding the psychocommunications revolution in the contemporary world. MR. NEVITT, after a distinguished career as an electronics engineer in Europe, South America, and North America, is now associated with the School of Business Administration at the University of Western Ontario and with the Centre for Culture and Technology. McLuhan and Nevitt have collaborated on a book, *Take Today: The Executive as Dropout* (New York, 1972).

The situation is complicated and its difficulties are enhanced by the impossibility of saying everything at once.[49]

In today's ECO-world of electric information that flows increasingly upon us from every side, we all encounter the predicament of *Alice in Wonderland.* Now effects merge with causes instantly through speedup, while "software" etherializes "hardware" by design.[50] All rigid distinctions between thinker and doer, observer and observed, object and subject are being eroded by the "rim-spin" of electric media. Old ground rules and human perceptions are being transformed by this new resonant surround where nothing is stable but change itself. But like water to a fish, the environment we live in remains hidden. Only children and artists see "the emperor's new clothes."

Continuity in Discontinuity

Today, metamorphosis by *chiasmus*—the reversal-of-process caused by increasing its speed, scope, or size—is visible everywhere for anyone to see. The chiasmus of speedup is slowdown. Perhaps first noted by ancient Chinese sages in *I Ching* or *The Book*

---

[49] R. T. Hersh citing Woodger on *Alice in Wonderland* in *American Scientist* (May-June, 1971): 293.

[50] "Software" is the organization of information for the shaping and metamorphosis of its "hardware" embodiment. The hardware/software relationship is not fixed, but is constantly changing in the process of "etherialization"—doing more and more with less and less.

of Changes, the history of chiastic patterns is traced through classical Greek and Hebrew literature by Nils W. Lund in *Chiasmus in the New Testament*.[51] Computer programmers have also learned that "information overload leads to pattern recognition" as breakdown becomes breakthrough: from "bits" to "bytes" to "whole" again.

Speeding up the components of any visually ordered structure or continuous space pattern will lead to breaking its connections and destroying its boundaries. They explode into the resonant gaps or interfaces that characterize the discontinuous structure of acoustic space. The visual perspective becomes an acoustic wraparound. Repetition of any visual pattern or modular form creates a mosaic with nonvisual effects, as the single photographic point of view becomes a multiple, iconic re-presentation. History becomes "mythic" through time-compression and juxtaposition of events as past, present, and future merge in electric *nowness*.

Novelty Causes Antiquity

Every innovation, whether of "hardware" product or "software" information, is an extension of man. Novelty becomes cliché through use. And constant use creates a new hidden environment while simultaneously pushing the old invisible ground into prominence, as a new figure, clearly visible for the first time. Every innovation scraps its immediate

[51] Nils Wilhelm Lund, *Chiasmus in the New Testament: A Study in Formgeschichte* (Chapel Hill: University of North Carolina Press, 1942).

predecessor and retrieves still older figures; it causes floods of antiques or nostalgic art forms and stimulates the search for "museum pieces." In such cliché-archetype patterns, the new continually recreates the old as novelty regenerates antiquity. Ancient cults and old jalopies are revived for "inner" satisfactions as we explore "outer" spaces. The motor car retrieved the countryside, scrapped the inner core of the city, and created suburban megalopolis. Invention is the mother of necessities, old and new.

Literacy Created Both Science and Causality

> *The royal divorce of thought and feeling.* [JAMES JOYCE]

Twenty-five centuries ago the Greeks invented Nature by abstracting it from total existence. They elevated their cosmos as an ordered figure upon the old ground of "chaotic" change. Since then, Western philosophers have looked upon the abstract figure of Greek Nature as their territory—an artificial ground which they have cut into conceptual figures that hide existence. Harold Innis was the first to demonstrate that Greek ability to separate "thinking" from "being" was due to their alphabetic writing. In *The Bias of Communication*[52] Innis traces this causal process through the gradual shift of sensory bias from the preliterate audile-tactile to the literate visual modes of

[52] Harold A. Innis, *The Bias of Communication* (Toronto: University of Toronto Press, 1964).

perception. Literacy became synonymous with Western civilization that divorced "subject' from "object" and thought from feeling, just as the dominant metaphors of mechanism widened the separation of "cause" and "effect."

In his analysis of *The Logic of Scientific Discovery*,[53] Karl R. Popper states:

> The "principle of causality" is the assertion that any event whatsoever can be causally explained—that it *can* be deductively predicted. According to the way in which one interprets the word "can" in this assertion, it will be either tautological (analytic), or else an assertion about reality (synthetic). For if "can" means that it is always logically possible to construct a causal explanation, then the assertion is tautological, since for any prediction whatsoever we can always find universal statements and initial conditions from which the prediction is derivable. (Whether these universal statements have been tested and corroborated in other cases is of course quite a different question.) If, however, "can" is meant to signify that the world is governed by strict laws, that it is so constructed that every specific event is an instance of a universal regularity or law, then the assertion is admittedly synthetic. But in this case it is not falsifiable, . . . I shall, therefore, neither adopt nor reject the "principle of causality"; I shall be content simply to exclude it, as "metaphysical," from the sphere of science.

---

[53] Karl R. Popper, *The Logic of Scientific Discovery* (New York: Basic Books, 1959): 39-40.

> I shall, however, propose a methodological rule which corresponds so closely to the "principle of causality" that the latter might be regarded as its metaphysical version. It is the simple rule that we are not to abandon the search for universal laws and for a coherent theoretical system, nor ever give up our attempts to explain causally any kind of event we can describe. This rule guides the scientific investigator in his work.

While exhorting scientists to continue "explaining" Nature as if by "causality," Popper proceeds to categorize it out of science into metaphysics via the "Vienna Circle." Unaware of the processes involved in discovering and transforming existence, Popper fails to consider the effects upon man himself of his own "hardware" and "software" extensions. There is unanimity among historians in presenting their subjects as figures without grounds.

Science Organizes Knowledge, Not Ignorance, Labels Rather than Processes

> *Love my label like myself.*
> [JAMES JOYCE]

Thomas Kuhn explains how scientists operate: One of the reasons why normal science seems to progress so rapidly is that its practitioners concentrate on "problems that only their own lack of ingenuity should keep them from solving."[54] And later, "Discovery comes with the awareness of anomaly, i.e. with the recognition that nature has somehow violated the paradigm-induced expectations that govern *normal science*."[55] Kuhn shows that the "paradigm of science" is the "medium" that transforms its "content" into normal science. But he remains oblivious of the much wider hidden ground of Western culture—the unconscious assumptions of visual psychic bias. He is unaware that the user is necessarily the "content" of any situation. Whereas the alphabet intensified by print "wrote off" existence, the "paradigm of science" has now become the cause of "normal science." Experiments designed to confirm the old normally conceal the new. *The medium is the message.*

George Bernard Shaw once tartly remarked that "every profession is a conspiracy against the laity." And Michael Polanyi recently added that "the principle of mutual control" ensures public recognition only to normal scientists, that is, conventional wisdom only. While supporting any scientist against every layman, "scientists watch over each other." Their hidden assumption is that a "field of systematic progress exists"—a never-ending upward progression from one step of the ladder of scientific knowledge to the next. Scientists defend their "cause" by mediated consensus—a "Skinner-box" that reinforces the

---

[54] Thomas S. Kuhn, *The Structure of Scientific Revolutions* (Chicago: University of Chicago Press, 1962), p. 37.
[55] Ibid.: 52.

"message." The new conventional wisdom is being seen, if not heard, at the annual convention.[56]

Erwin Chargaff describes the dilemma facing every pioneer—"either to *understand* the world or to *explain* it":

> The natural scientist is often faced with a series of observations, a set of phenomena, into which he attempts subsequently to introduce some sort of chronological or causal order. He determines several points and connects them to a curve; he measures certain values in a number of samples and estimates the averages and deviations; he constructs a reaction chain or postulates a cycle: whatever he does, there remains much darkness between the few points of light. Whether he emphasizes the light or dwells on the obscurities will depend upon his temperament, but even more upon the temper of the times and upon a form of everchanging vogue or fashion which acts as a censor forbidding him to be ahead by more than one or two steps. If he runs too fast, he disappears from our sight; if he goes too slowly, he joins the 18th century. For most people, this is not a problem: they are where all the others are.[57]

Professor Chargaff is here illuminating the obsession of scientists with concepts. And Donald A. Schon notes that "the tendency either to obscurantize or to explain away novelty reflects the great difficulty of explaining it. The difficulty comes in large part from

---

[56] Michael Polanyi, *The Tacit Dimension* (Garden City, NY, 1967), pp. 71-72.
[57] Erwin Chargaff, "Preface to a Grammar of Biology," *Science* 172: 3984 (1971): 638.

our inclination, with things and thought alike, to take an after-the-fact view."[58] What the scientist normally sees is either a replay of past scientific experience or an up-and-coming threat in his "rear-view mirror." Coming events cast their shadows before them? Don't look back; they may be gaining on you!

Causality as Probe, Not Program

Mario Bunge concludes his study of causality by saying:

> There is no necessary relation between causality and prediction, any more than there is between causality and explanation.[59] . . . The causal principle reflects or reconstructs only a few aspects of determination. Reality is much too rich to be compressible once and for all into a framework of categories elaborated during an early stage of rational knowledge, which consequently cannot account for the whole variety of types of determination . . . . What has been rejected in this book is not the principle of causation, but its unlimited extrapolation, as asserted by the doctrine of causalism, or causal determinism. . . . The causal principle is, in

[58] Donald Alan Schon, *Displacement of Concepts* (London: Tavistock Publications, 1963).

[59] Mario Bunge, *Causality: The Place of the Causal Principle in Modern Science* (Cambridge: Harvard University Press, 1959), p. 332.

> short, . . . a general hypothesis subsumed under the universal principle of determinacy, and having an approximate validity in its proper domain.[60]

The "causality" concept may serve either as a "package" for old experience or as a "probe" for new knowledge. The meaning of "causality" is determined, not by definition as an isolated figure, but by what it does in re-cognizing process patterns in the ground of existence.

Causality Is Tested by Experience as Percept, Not Concept

> *To most men, experience is like the stern lights of a ship, which illumine only the track it has passed.* [SAMUEL T. COLERIDGE]

Mario Bunge explains that, according to Hegel, "cause and effect are but the two poles of the interaction category, which 'realizes the causal relation in its complete development.' Besides, in Hegel's system of objective idealism, the category of interaction enjoyed an ontological status, whereas Kant had treated it, alongside the remaining categories, as a purely epistemological element, and even as prior to experience. . . . Hegel held nature in

[60] Ibid.: 352-53.

contempt,"[61] Karl Marx and Friederich Engels, who were Hegel's pupils, stood on his toes rather than on his shoulders. They turned Hegelian dialectics upside down by postulating the primacy of "matter-in-motion" asymptotically reflected by mental processes. Their ambitious aim was "not merely to *understand* the world but to *change* it." They proclaimed human "experience" as the sole arbiter and the ultimate test of any "truth" whatever. But in "testing" their "truths" via dialectical materialism, they ignored the hidden ground underlying all their figures of "experience"—the visual assumptions of Western "sciences" and "humanities" alike.

In his *Dialectics of Nature*, Engels outlines the Marxian concept of causality:

> The first thing that strikes us in considering matter in motion is the interconnection of the individual motions of separate bodies, their *being determined* by one another. But not only do we find that a particular motion is followed by another, we find also that we can evoke a particular motion by setting up the conditions in which it takes place in nature, indeed that we can produce motions which do not occur at all in nature (industry), at least not in this way, and that we can give these motions a predetermined direction and extent. *In this way*, by the *activity of human beings*, the idea of *causality* becomes established, the idea that one motion is the *cause* of another. True, the regular sequence of certain natural phenomena can by itself give rise to the idea of causality: the heat and light that come with the sun; but this affords no

---

[61] Ibid.: 161, 201.

proof, and to that extent Hume's skepticism was correct in saying that a regular *post hoc* can never establish a *propter hoc. But the activity of human beings forms the test of causality.* If we bring the sun's rays to a focus by means of a lens and make them act like the rays of an ordinary fire, we thereby prove that the heat comes from the sun. If we bring together in a rifle the priming, the explosive charge, and the bullet and then fire it, we count upon the effect known in advance from previous experience, because we can follow in all its details the whole process of ignition, combustion, explosion by the sudden conversion into gas and pressure of the gas on the bullet. And here the skeptic cannot even say that because of previous experience it does not follow that it will be the same next time. For, as a matter of fact, it does sometimes happen that it is *not* the same, that the priming or the gunpowder fails to work, that the barrel bursts, etc. But it is precisely this which *proves* causality instead of refuting it, because we can find out the cause of each such deviation from the rule by appropriate investigation: chemical decomposition of the priming, dampness, etc., of the gunpowder, defect in the barrel, etc., etc., so that here the *test of causality* is so to say a *double* one.

Natural science, like philosophy, has hitherto entirely neglected the influence of men's activity on their thought; both know only nature on the one hand and thought on the other. But it is *precisely the alteration of nature by men, not solely nature as such, which is the most essential and immediate basis of human*

> *thought, and it is in the measure that man has learned to change nature that his intelligence has increased.* The naturalistic conception of history, as found, for instance, to a greater or lesser extent in Draper and other scientists, as if nature exclusively reacts on man, and natural conditions everywhere exclusively determined his historical development, is therefore one-sided and *forgets that man also reacts on nature, changing it, and creating new conditions of existence for himself.* There is damned little left of "nature" as it was in Germany at the time when the Germanic peoples immigrated into it. The earth's surface, climate, vegetation, fauna, and the human beings themselves have continually changed, and all this owing to human activity, while the changes of nature in Germany which have occurred in the process of time without human interference are incalculably small.[62]

And he continues:

> *Reciprocal action* is the first thing that we encounter when we consider matter in motion as a whole from the standpoint of modern natural science. We see a series of forms of motion, mechanical motion, heat, light, electricity, magnetism, chemical union and decomposition, transitions of states of aggregation, organic life, all of which, if *at present* we *still* make an exception of organic life, pass into one another, mutually determine one another, are in one place cause and in

[62] Friedrich Engels and C. P. Dutt, *Dialectics of Nature* trans. J. B. S. Haldane (New York: International Publishers, 1940): 170-72.

> another effect, the sum-total of the motion in all its changing forms remaining the same (Spinoza: *substance is causa sui*—strikingly expresses the reciprocal action). Mechanical motion becomes transformed into heat, electricity, magnetism, light, etc., and *vice-versa*. Thus natural science confirms . . . that reciprocal action is the true *causa finalis* of things. We cannot go back further than to knowledge of this reciprocal action, for the very reason that there is nothing behind to know.[63]

"This music is worse than it sounds," for it is played literally by *eye* without *ear*. Although its epistemology is dialectical, its ontology still rests on abstract Greek Nature. Marx and Engels saw conflicts of old figures as creating grounds for each other while they remained oblivious of the new information surround that had transformed their assumptions. They were attempting to *match* the concepts of an earlier age to the experience newly visible in the "rear-view-mirror" of the 19th century. They were unaware that *percepts of existence always lie behind concepts of Nature*. Their hidden hang-up was the visual bias of all "objectivity," whether "materialist" or "idealist." They also ignored the acoustic "message of the birds"—the output of any process, biological or psychic, always differs qualitatively from the input. There are no "through-puts" or connections between processes but only gaps or interfaces for "keeping in touch" with "where the action is." When the "play" between the wheel and the axle ends, so does the wheel. While the "subjectivist" puts on the world as his own clothes, the "objectivist" supposes that he can stand naked "out of this world." The ideal of the

---

63 Ibid.: 173.

rationalist philosophers still persists: to achieve an inclusive "science of the sciences." But such a science would be a monster of preconceived figures minus unperceived grounds. No "objective" dialectics of Nature or of science as visually ex-plainable can stand up to a resonant interface with the existential. For "testing the truth" is not merely matching by congruence or classification; it is making sense out of the totality of experience—a process of pattern re-cognition that requires not only concepts but active perception by all the senses. Today, as "hardware" is transmuted into pure information by the process of "etherialization," the "inner" and the "outer" merge—thinking becomes doing.

The "Stereophonic" Perspective of Ear and Eye

But at my back I alwais hear
Times winged Charriot hurrying near:
And yonder all before us lye
Desarts of vast Eternity.
[ANDREW MARVELL, *To His Coy Mistress*]

In the 16th century, as words went "visual" they lost their "resoun" or metamorphic resonance and became mere "rabble." Only "artists" like William Shakespeare and Andrew Marvell were aware of the "double perspective" of hearing behind and seeing ahead. Scientists like Robert Boyle turned away from ancient books "to get in touch" again through ancient crafts. Their successors went from libraries to laboratories and pushed on to "reason" without "rhyme." Early perspective was toward the viewer and began to recede only in the Renaissance. Today television begins perspective back toward the viewer again. The reversal of sensory stress from *eye* to *ear* via media is perceived by "artists" like James Joyce and T. S. Eliot as an opportunity for consciously retrieving reason, rhyme, and rhythm:

STOP

LOOK

LISTEN

The visual metaphors of science have had the effect of translating totalities of process relations into mere connections between separate phenomena, or things. John Stuart Mill wrote: "The Law of Causation ... is but the familiar truth that invariability of succession is found by observation to obtain between every fact in nature and some other fact which has preceded it . . . . The invariable antecedent is termed the cause. The invariable consequent, the effect."[64] Pushed to extreme, the fragmented features of abstract Nature exclude the ground of actual nature. But always the action is in the gap. There are no "things," only processes.

Whereas "reality" in the 19th century was to match the old, "reality" in the 20th century is to make the new. Since Werner Heisenberg and Linus Pauling,[65] the only remaining material bond is

---

64 John Stuart Mill, *A System of Logic*, 9th ed. (London: Longmans, Green, Reader, and Dyer, 1875): 376.

65 In *The Nature of the Chemical Bond and the Structures of Molecules and Crystals: An Introduction to Modern Chemistry*, 3rd ed. (Ithaca, NY: Cornell University Press, 1960), Linus Pauling establishes that the chemical bond is not a mere connection but a "stabilization of the system of resonance energy."

resonance. All physical, psychic and social processes merge in constant play and replay. There are no more spectators in lab or life, only participants in the Global Electric Theatre. Sputnik created a new proscenium arch that transformed our awareness of planet Polluto—a limited figure against the ground of limitless space. The Apollo age has scrapped Greek Nature as we assume full responsibility for orchestrating our total environment on human scales beyond ideologies.

Effects Precede Causes

> *The child is father to the man*
> [WILLIAM WORDSWORTH]

The father and the family make the child, just as the child remakes them in a continuing process. Like families, all grounds are a totality of cumulative effects that continually gell into figures as causes. "When the time is ripe" in any process, the effects as ground have preceded the cause as figures. "*Causality*" *is a process pattern, exposed by discovery or imposed by invention.* The effects are consciously made accessible either through discovery or invention as new causes, both "hardware" and "software." For example, while tracing the development of American agriculture, Siegfried Giedion observes that "phenomena often regarded solely as the outcome of mechanization had already appeared before the mechanization took effect."[66] Similarly, many of the

[66] Siegfried Giedion, *Mechanization Takes Command* (New York: Oxford University Press, 1948): 168.

effects of the telephone had been anticipated by the general speedup of information that centered in the telegraph. The effects of "wireless" were anticipated by earlier technologies of wire and cable. Road traffic had been steadily accelerating before the advent of the railroad. A general environmental speedup preceded the development of the airways. The new effects through new uses of any innovation are realized only after it becomes obsolescent through fresh innovation. The old hidden ground then emerges as a new rear-view figure for all to see. Computers are still serving mainly as agents to sustain precomputer effects.

In the broader context of *The Hidden Face*, Ida F. Goerres observes that "those who experience great historical changes at first hardly notice them, only the fact that they are being dragged along, willy-nilly; some time must always elapse before such changes pierce to the deeper levels of consciousness and engender new attitudes, new modes of behaviour."[67] Conceptual formulation, whether in "software" or "hardware," always lags behind "where it's at."

Effects Are Perceived Whereas Causes are Conceived

Unable to explore actual processes perceptually from every side, the conceptual man apprehends only visual goals. For example, the conventional ideas of

[67] Ida Friederike Goerres, The Hidden Face: A Study of St. Therese of Lisieux (New York: Pantheon, 1959): 24.

"evolution" and "technology" are illusions engendered by the visual bias of literate cultures. Such cultures translated the "chain of being" metaphor from the astral to the biological plane. For the use of the "missing link" idea we are indebted to a missing inventor. So far nobody has appeared as originator of this phrase. The gap created by the "missing link" has sparked more exploration and discovery than the established links in "connected" science. Conceptual choices, like "natural selection," can come only after the fact. The "origins" of all species vanish in rear-view perspectives, while the music goes round and round.

Causality is Not Merely Reciprocal Action but Complementary Process

Nils Bohr's complementarity that represents "atomic" interactions as both "acoustic" waves and "visual" particles is exemplified by every process involving the continuous interplay of simultaneous actions. (All "elementary particles" are packaged ignorance.) Aristotle's "pairs," where one process is always the privation of another, were also familiar to the Chinese sage Wang Fu (A. D. 90-165): "Poverty arises from wealth, weakness derives from power./ Order engenders disorder, and security insecurity."[68] That is, affluence breeds poverty (not physical

[68] Cited by Etienne Balazs in *Chinese Civilization and Bureaucracy: Variations on a Theme* (New Haven, CT: Yale University Press, 1964).

hardship) and learning causes ignorance (not less information), just as matter creates space (not void). Such complementarity of figure-ground appears as a causal relation in all "prepackaged" processes. *Complementarity is the process whereby effects become causes.* Today, as causes and effects merge instantaneously, the new common ground is neither container nor category but the vastness of space via media.

Explanations East or West?

> *What we cannot speak about we must confine to silence.* [L. WITTGENSTEIN]

What most scientists still fail to perceive is the "visual" bias of logical inference imposed by Western civilization itself. What constitutes a fact or an adequate explanation? Mario Bunge writes:

> Most scientists are prepared to grant that the chief theoretical (that is, nonpragmatic) aim of scientific research is to answer, in an intelligible, exact, and testable way, five kinds of questions, namely, those beginning with *what* (or *how*), *where*, *when*, *whence*, and *why*. . . . The Five W's of Science. (Only radical empiricists deny that science has an explanatory function, and restrict the task of scientific research to the description and prediction of observable phenomena.) Also, most scientists would agree that all five W's are gradually (and painfully) being answered through the establishment of scientific *laws*, that is, general

> hypotheses about the patterns of being and becoming.[69]

The poet Ezra Pound understood that the telegraphic mosaic of news items and headlines was an organization of experience that bridged the ancient Oriental and Western forms. In his *ABC of Reading*,[70] Pound cites an essay by Ernest Fenollosa:

> In Europe, if you ask a man to define anything, his definition always moves away from the simple things that he knows perfectly well, it recedes into an unknown region of remoter and progressively remoter abstraction.
>
> Thus if you ask him what red is, he says it is a "colour."
>
> If you ask him what a colour is, he tells you it is a vibration or reflection of light, or a division of the spectrum. And if you ask him what vibration is, he tells you it is a mode of energy, or something of that sort, until you arrive at a modality of being, or non-being, or at any rate you get in beyond your depth, and beyond his depth . . . . But when the Chinaman wanted ... to define red ... how did he go about it?
>
> He ... put together the abbreviated pictures of
>
> ROSE CHERRY
>
> IRON RUST FLAMINGO
>
> ... the Chinese "word" or ideogram for red is based on something everyone *knows*.

---

69 Bunge: 248.

70 Ezra Pound, *ABC of Reading* (New York: J. Laughlin, New Directions Paperback No. 89, 1960): 19-22.

Explanations that ignore the perceptual complementarity of *eye* and *ear* lead to conceptual conflict—the divorce of "rhyme and reason." "I have often seen it said," repeats the specialist. "Speak that I may see thee," said the seer.

Every language creates an all-pervasive hidden environment of services. And words themselves are metaphors (Greek *meta-pherein*: carry across) that transform meaning by translating one form of being into another. The semanticist ideal—one word for one meaning—has already been achieved by "yes-or-no" computer languages. Whereas computer programmers try to reduce the infinite variety of the world to the two-bit wit of their machines, "artists" like James Joyce can create universes of resonant meaning out of two words: the "orb urbs" and the "urb orbs."

Making Sense

> *Poetry can communicate before it is understood.* [T. S. ELIOT]

The *eye* makes a "visual space structure" with individual points of view or centers and definite margins or boundaries—everything in its proper place and time. Each of our senses makes its own space, but no sense can function in isolation. Only as sight relates to touch, or kinesthesia, or sound, can the eye see. In isolation, the visual sense presents an immediate blur—all ground minus figures. The bridging of the senses creates an interface of figure-ground relations that make sense. Making sense is never matching or mere one-to-one correspondence which is an assumption of visual bias. For the *ear* makes an "acoustic space structure" with centers everywhere and margins nowhere, like a musical surround or the boundless universe. Making sense involves "unified sensibility" or *synesthesia*, as E. H. Gombrich explains in *Art and Illusion*:

> What is called "synesthesia," the splashing over of impressions from one sense modality to another, is a fact to which all languages testify. They work both ways—from sight to sound and from sound to sight. We speak of loud colors or of bright sounds, and everyone knows what we mean. Nor are the ear and the eye the only senses that are thus converging to a common center. There is touch in such terms as "velvety voice" and "a cold light," taste with "sweet harmonies" of colors or sounds, and so on through countless permutations . . . . Representation is never a replica. The forms of art, ancient and modern, are not duplications of what the artist has in mind any more than they are duplications of what he sees in the outer world. In both cases they are renderings within an acquired medium, a medium grown up through tradition and skill—that of the artist and that of the beholder . . . . Synesthesia concerns relationships.[71]

Relevant to the great gap between program "content" and the effect of the medium itself is the approach to the image in J. Isaacs' *Background of Modern Poetry*: "'The exact word,' says Mr. Aldington,

---

[71] E. H. Gombrich, *Art and Illusion: A Study in the Psychology of Pictorial Representation* (New York: Pantheon Books, 1965): 366-370.

'does not mean the word which exactly describes the object itself, it means the exact word which brings the effect of that object before the reader as it presented itself to the poet's mind at the time of writing the poem."[72] Apropos the linguistic studies of N. Chomsky, Thomas S. Kuhn, philosopher of science, was recently cited by the *Listener* on "what people are prepared to accept as facts at one point cease to be and new things are regarded as facts."[73] Our studies of media as environments that alter patterns of perception and sensibility are intended to develop awareness of the process by which "new things" come to be regarded as "facts." These "new facts" concern the message or effects of new media as hidden environments. These effects are not the "content" of the media. The content is always the "hypocrite lecteur" (or *auditeur*). This is the central fact missing from the speculations of Noam Chomsky concerning the verbal universe. Languages are not programs but environments which are hidden from the young learner, and to which, like fish to water, he relates synesthetically, using all his faculties at once. After childhood the senses specialize via the channels of dominant technologies and weaponries. Electric channels of information have the effect of reducing (or elevating) people to the discarnate status of instant information.

The Artist Precedes the Scientist

[72] J. Isaacs, *The Background of Modern Poetry* (New York: Dutton, 1952): 45.
[73] (July 27, 1971): 142.

The first principle of evidence is that things have to be approached on their own terms if any understanding is to be attained. Edgar Allan Poe was the first to stress the need to begin with effects and to work backwards, in poetry and in detective fiction alike. Just as Poe provided clues for ascending from *The Maelstrom*, Beckett replays not waiting, but the effects of the experience of waiting, in *Waiting for Godot*. In *Four Quartets* T. S. Eliot studies effects as causes: "In my end is my beginning." And Wyndham Lewis noted that "the artist is engaged in writing a detailed history of the future because, older than the fish, he alone can live in the inclusive present." In symbolist art, connections are deliberately pulled out in order to involve the public in a creative role. In symbolist statement, the ground is suppressed in order to highlight the figure. A boot lying on a highway is a symbol; a tire is not, for the medium can reverse the roles of producer and consumer by making the reader or audience not only the "content" but the comaker of the work. Movies and television are antithetic.

When we say "the medium is the message," we suppress the fact that the user or audience or cognitive agent is both the "content" and maker of the experience, in order to highlight the effects of the medium or the hidden environment or ground of the experience. The 19th century, as the first great consumer age, suppressed the function of the user and the public as cognitive agent and producer. The pre-Raphaelites at least strove to overcome the passive consumer bias of an industrial time by stressing the role of work and crafts in art and society. They tried to have some relevance to their time by playing down the consumer role and scorning the easy package method that had grown up in the arts and industry alike. In his time, John Donne strove for relevance to his "hypocrite lecteurs" by constructing for them a broken and discontinuous discourse. He was seeking nonlineal and non-19th-century effects "to trouble the understanding, to displace, and discompose and disorder the judgement . . . or to empty it of former apprehensions, and to shake beliefs, with which it had possessed itself before, and then, when it is thus melted, to poure it into new molds, when it is thus mollified, to stamp and imprint new forms, and new opinions on it." Donne's "Attic" or "curt" and broken style not only ruffled the feathers of the 19th-century establishment, but appeals to contemporary minds in our own century.

In 1903, W. B. Yeats, meditating on the "emotion of multitude," explained that it is achieved by a discontinuous parallel between two actions; "I have been wondering why I dislike the clear and logical construction which seems necessary if one is to succeed on the modern stage . . . . The Greek drama has got the emotion of multitude from its chorus . . . to witness as it were, some well ordered fable . . . . The Shakespearean drama gets the emotion of multitude out of the sub-plot which copies the main plot, much as a shadow upon the wall copies one's body in the firelight. We think of King Lear less as the history of one man and his sorrows than as the history of a whole evil time." Depth awareness is created by parallel suggestion, not by connected statement. Yeats's observation can also be found in Bacon, who writes on the modes of aphorism as contrasted with "writing in Method," in his *Advancement of Learning*: "Aphorisms, representing a knowledge broken, do invite men to inquire farther; whereas Methods, carrying the show of a total, do secure men, as if they were at farthest." Even the ad agencies know that to sell a car or a coat they must present the satisfactions in figure-ground relationship that will create the desired psychic effects. They would not show a coat in relation to naked natives nor a car in a world without roads. The 19th-century consumer preference is not relevant to the electric age of quantum physics, even though our media bureaucracies continue to produce mainly consumer packages. But every specialist has a stake in his own knowledge, just as every conventional man has the right to defend his own ignorance.

Causality as Making the New

What Western philosophers, right, left, and center, have continued to ignore is that *matching* the old excludes *making* the new. Concepts always follow percepts. In fact they are a kind of ossification of percepts—endlessly repeated percepts which frequently obscure invention and innovation.

The entire obsession of our age with *existentialism* has been based on the awareness that concept is not percept. One can have numerous classifications that do not correspond to one's actual experience. We are often smothered in images of ourselves and of others that do not correspond to "presences." The Western world has built up a vast apparatus of classifications as a means of controlling and harmonizing experience. These have tended to be colossal systems of concepts which prevent us from direct encounter with ourselves and our world: they constitute the "rear-view mirror." But "existentialism" pushed to extreme as a figure loses touch with the ground of existence itself.

The Renaissance made a clean sweep of the vast methodologies and dialectics of scholastic disputation. Today, we are making a clean sweep of all the merely private points of view achieved through five centuries of intense individualism. Inevitably, in these cathartic conditions, many babies are thrown out with little bath water. Enormous destruction seems to accompany such periods of discovery and innovation. The ordinary flood of effects that pour from ill-conceived courses of action swamp perception.

Scientific "objectivity," like Othello's "ocular proof," is an optical illusion of truth. The testimony of the blind Frenchman Jacques Lusseyran is relevant here:

> When I came across the myth of objectivity in certain modern writers, it made me angry. So there was only one world for these people, the same for everyone. And all the other worlds were to be counted as illusions left over from the past. Or why not call them by their name—hallucinations? I had to learn to my cost how wrong they were.
>
> From my experience I knew that it was enough to take from a man a memory here, an association there, to deprive him of hearing or sight, for the world to undergo immediate transformation, and for another world, entirely different but entirely coherent to be born. Another world? Not really. The same world, rather, but seen from another angle, and counted in entirely new measures. When this happened, all the hierarchies they called objective

> were turned upside down, scattered to the four winds, not even like theories but like whims.[74]

"Objectivity" is achieved by matching new observations with old concepts by specialist observers doubly isolated from existence by abstract Nature on the one hand, and controlled laboratory environments on the other. No dog from the streets will behave in accordance with the stimulus-response figures of "conditioned reflexes" until conditioned by a Pavlovian ground. The laboratory is the hidden environment of effects that make the causes possible.

Predicting What Has Already Happened By Being the First to Perceive It

Displacing percepts is the role of the artist. The artist in any field is the person who anticipates the effects in his own times. The art of remaking the world eternally new is achieved by careful and deliberate dislocation of ordinary perceptions. Even the surrealist had this ambition—to attain a fresh vision of the world by the juxtaposition of ordinary things, for example, the "fur-lined teacup" and "Mona Lisa's moustache." Scientists make their discoveries as "artists," not specialists. Such scientists construct experiments as "works of art" to probe the environment. But anyone with enough vitality to

---

74 Jacques Lusseyran, *And There Was Light* (Boston: Little, Brown, 1963): 143-44.

confront the actual through direct perception can predict the future by noting what has already happened. For the future of the future is the present.

The breakdown or hang-up is always in the connection, whereas the breakthrough or discovery is inside the problem itself, not outside but "in the gap." Breakdown is the old cause in action, the extension of the old figure to the new ground. Breakthrough is the effect of the understanding as the new cause. The solution is a figure that we can discover by organizing our ignorance and swarming over the ground. This process is encapsulated in the myth of Hercules in the Augean stables.

Causality on Both Sides of the Looking Glass

As the mathematician Charles Dodgson (Lewis Carroll), romping with *Alice in Wonderland*, explains while playing hitherside of the glass in Logic-land "'Contrariwise,' continued Tweedledee, 'if it was so, it might be; and if it were so, it would be; but as it isn't, it ain't. That's logic.'" And while playing thitherside in Echo-land: "Now, *here*, you see, it takes all the running *you* can do, to stay in the same place. If you want to get somewhere else, you must run at least twice as fast as that!" Today, all barriers have gone with the ether as we live on both sides of the looking glass.

Understanding is Neither a Point of View nor a Value Judgment

Lewis Carroll makes inventories of effects as causes that relate modes of dynamic perception. They are neither definitions of concepts nor expressions of opinion, since all patterns of perception merge and metamorphose in the very act of exploration and discovery. They avoid value judgments, and serve as guides to insight and to comprehension through *re-cognition* of the *dynamic structures* that occur in all processes. In replaying such patterns we are not taking any side but many sides, also the *inside.*

Today's Causality Program's Evitable Fate

At electric speeds, new direct perception of existence by-passes old die-hard concepts of Nature. We can now anticipate the effects—both services and disservices—before allowing the causes to develop. We no longer merely choose options, we make them. We can invent the remedies for both fortune and misfortune. Today, causing and explaining and predicting merge while teacher-student, consumer-producer, and audience-actor unite in new roles for the Global Electric Theatre. The future is not what it used to be; neither is causality, for thought travels much faster and farther than light.

Comment: Effects Precede Causes by Joseph Owens[75]

This dictum can hardly be accepted or rejected on the basis of anything patently obvious. If it could, it would not justify proposal as a topic for serious comment. It requires scrutiny in the infinitely expansive panorama suggested by the Wordsworth quote, "The child is father to the man." To have the right meaning here, "child" has to include the totality of environment and culture as well as all the activities and formative influence of early years, with a host of intangibles that reach back far beyond the Precambrian Era in time, and in space to the plunging sweep of the outer galaxies. All that and more goes into fathering a man, and makes imperative a rather elevated viewpoint for correctly assessing the present topic.

The ostentatiously obvious meanings of cause and effect are accordingly not the main issue. Obviously, to start a car one turns on the ignition and feeds the gas. One does not in some unimaginable way first suppose a started car and then expect it to insert the key and fill up the tank. Here one cannot show the

75 In the original publication in *Technology and Culture*, the following author identification appeared: REV. OWENS, C. St. R., is professor of philosophy at the University of Toronto and senior fellow at the Pontifical Institute of Mediaeval Studies in Toronto. He is the author of many books and articles, principally on Aristotelian and Thomistic metaphysics.

movie reel backward. In these obvious matters one follows the time arrow down a one-way street. The traffic law is strictly enforced. For practical purposes one regards these causes as preceding the effects.

But one-way streets are not the only type of traffic arteries. In fact, they are ad hoc devices for convenience in a hemmed-in situation. In a broader perspective the superhighways present long parallel streams moving in opposite direction. So do cause and effect function from a correspondingly higher viewpoint. The construction of one's dream home, carefully planned for years and put down in detail by the architect on the blueprints, proceeds by feeding the designs into brick and woodwork and metal as the workmen slowly bring the house into material being. The house, the final effect, keeps exercising its causality on the work, while *pari passu* the work produces the house. The streams run parallel in opposite directions. In one way, the effect is tellingly preceding the cause, in the manner in which the goal is everywhere the cause of the efforts to attain it. Simultaneously, the goal is the effect that those efforts are bringing into existence.

These two observations are well known and uncontested. Neither can be what is meant in any blanket assertion that effects precede causes, if the statement is really significant. What is intended seems much more profound. It is what appears when things are viewed not from the surface levels of either one-way streets or superhighways, but in the complexity of all traffic levels from the lowest to highest in the airport control tower. Could it be what Aristotle had in mind when he observed: "Those who suppose, as the Pythagoreans and Speusippus do, that supreme beauty and goodness are not present in the beginning, because the beginnings both of plants and of animals are *causes*, but beauty and completeness are in the *effects* of these, are wrong in their opinion. For the seed comes from other individuals which are prior and complete, and the first thing is not seed but the complete being."[76]

The setting in which this statement was made was all inclusive. Both nature and heaven depend upon something that is entirely and eternally actual.[77] The ultimate completion and perfection are accordingly not something to be worked out by a cause. Rather, it is something that is there in its finished and complete perfection before there can be any question of a cause going to work. Perfection is what comes first. It is already there. Progress toward it on the temporal level is subsequent. The effects therefore precede their causes. The reason given is cogent. Actuality is more than potentiality. The mere potentiality of a thing in its causes is not enough to account for its actuality in the real world. The effects must therefore in their actuality precede the activity of their causes. Greek thought was adamant in its adherence to the principle that nothing comes from nothing.

In the Christian context these considerations stand out still more sharply. From Saint Paul[78] through Dionysius,[79] the notion that all things exist eternally in God was handed down with enthusiasm. It was strikingly developed against the Aristotelian background in the course of the 13th century. These effects preexist and are pre-contained long before the causes that produce them go into operation. In advance pure actuality, now identified with the unique God of Christian revelation, contains in actual

---

[76] *Metaphysics* 12.1072b30-1073al (Oxford translation).
[77] Ibid.: b7-30.
[78] Colossians 1:17.
[79] *On the Divine Names* c.V.

existence all effects and all the perfections of these effects. It contains them completely. They are there, in existence, from the start. In the pure actuality of God all the effects have their basic existence, eternally and perfectly. For this reason they likewise precede in essence, eternally, their production by causes in time. Only subsequently, as Aquinas explains,[80] do the effects have existence in themselves and in human knowledge.

Clearly enough, then, from the viewpoint of Christian thinking, the effects in full existence precede the temporal causes that produce them. As existent in pure actuality the effects are strictly identical with their eternally abiding cause. On this humanly incomprehensible level the question whether effects precede causes or vice versa is meaningless and cannot methodically be asked. When asked, it refers to the situation open to the broadest sweep of observation and deduction. On this radar screen, on which the air levels as well as the ground level of traffic are made manifest simultaneously, the effects are shown to be eternally preexistent while their production is seen taking place in time. From the vantage point of the control tower, the best perspective available to the human mind, the effects undoubtedly precede the causes.

These reflections may send a cold chill down the marrow of the process philosophers and the progressivists. The perfection men strive so hard to achieve has been in existence long before their efforts. Nor is the world keyed to imperfection, anxiety, nausea, and despair, as the existentialists of the thirties and forties would have it. On the contrary, perfection is present from the outset. This is a truth that needs to be faced. It may be hard on fatuity and

---

[80] *Qodlibets* 8.1c.

vanity, but it does not dampen initiative nor cool enthusiasm. To bring into existence in the temporal order what is already preexistent in the eternal is no mean achievement. The accompanying knowledge that the perfection now sought after actually exists on a higher level need not dim the luster of the effort. Rather, this knowledge is encouraging and stimulating, for it shows that one is not pursuing a chimera. The terse formulation, "Effects precede causes," has the merit of giving vivid expression to a philosophically important truth.

Comment: Through a Rearview Mirror—Darkly by Frederick D. Wilhelmsen[81]

Once there was a lady named Bright
Who could travel faster than light
She went out one day
In a relative way
And came back the previous night.

Presumably, the "previous night" is the figure or cause itself produced by the effect, "the day"—today—ground of Lady Bright's experience. "Traveling faster than light in a relative way" would be the medium of

---

[81] In the original publication in *Technology and Culture*, the following author identification appeared: DR. WILHELMSEN, professor of philosophy and politics at the University of Dallas (Irving, Texas), is the author of *The War on Man: Media and Machines* and, with Jane Bret, of *Telepolitics*.

its own message. Lady Bright is the content or user of this Alice in Wonderland wandering.

I have no intention in the space afforded me of attempting an exegesis of the essay by Marshall McLuhan and Barrington Nevitt. Dr. McLuhan's writing is contrived to make people think, not match up his conclusions with their own. This misunderstanding about the Master of Media's intentions lies behind the often unfriendly attacks directed against him in Rosenthal's collection, *McLuhan: Pro and Con.*[82] I shall, rather, direct to McLuhan/Nevitt the following question and then run with the ball myself. If, "when the time is ripe in any process, the effects as ground have preceded the cause as figure," if "*Causality is a process pattern, exposed by discovery or imposed by invention,*" if, further, "effects are consciously made accessible either through discovery or invention as new causes," where do we *initially* discover the cart which is before the horse?

The question imposes itself upon us as a result of the massive attack launched by David Hume against the so-called principle of causality. Hume could experience visually the shock of billiard ball A upon billiard ball B, but he could visually experience the action of one ball causing the action of the other. "Causation" cannot be visualized: therefore it must be banished from science! Hume never denied causality (efficient causality, to use Aristotelian language) as a human experience, as a process lived and *done*, exercised, by all men. He merely banished that experience from the realm of science and domesticated it within the somewhat dubious order of "faith."

---

82 Raymond Rosenthal, ed. *McLuhan: Pro and Con* (New York: Funk & Wagnalls, 1968).

We have no "vision"—conceptual or ocular—of causality at all. Hume was dead right on this point. But we do have an initial experience of causality from which anything else we might know or think we know about the business takes its point of departure. We live causality as an act performed when we reason and when we will. Let us set aside the act of willing and thus avoid the knotty problems circling around freedom and determinism. Let us move directly to the act of reasoning, "thinking things out" to their conclusions. It is a safe assumption that science, hence science's relation to causality, is patterned within a human act or operation that most men would recognize as "reasonable." Crazy men, at least *qua* crazy, do not do science. When I reason, "the child"—whatever goes into the conclusion—is made by "the father"—the man concluding, the personally achieved "Eureka Point" of Archimedes, the "I've got it!"—and is made simultaneously by "the child."

Every original thinker, even the most modest in his pretensions to creativity, is at least mildly irritated when a bright student immediately grasps a conclusion that it took him years to come by. The stock response—"Why doesn't everybody see that?"—fails to assuage vanity offended. The conclusion—invention, discovery, breakthrough—was not all that obvious *before* he thought it out for himself. Had his insight been so evident, he would have known it before he knew it! The rearview mirror, the after-the-fact once set up by the mind's activity, is the moment of determinism within the total structure of invention. In terms of classical Aristotelian logic, the premises do "cause" the conclusion. The conclusion flows "necessarily" from the premises. This is the cart before the horse about which McLuhan/Nevitt are talking, I do believe.

> The conclusion that the angles of a triangle are equal to two right angles is not contained in the definition of a triangle. Nor is it contained in the notion of a parallel line drawn through the apex. But these two notions when taken together result in the new knowledge contained in the conclusion. Both logic and mathematics, accordingly may be regarded as creative in their activity.[83]

But what Owens says of logic and mathematics is true of even the most banal act of reasoning. The "intelligibility" or "thinkability" or "meaning" of discovery or invention emerges as a figure which "causes" its own ground, the affirmation that the conclusion is true, is so. From this point of view, but only from this point of view, the history of science and technology looks like an iron chain—not of being, but of meaning—which unfolds logically through time, one set of conclusions functioning as points of departure which engender new conclusions, a new technology unfolding from a previous technology. Hegelian and Marxist determinism depend on this manner of understanding human history. Evolutionary or progressivist philosophy of history sees the history of science in terms analogous to the story of the butterfly. Everything new is already given in the past, at least as promise or hidden potentiality. Man backs into the future with his eyes glued on the past.

But it takes only a moment's reflection to understand that the internal combustion engine did not evolve out of the horse, that Fulton's steamboat did not bring forth potentialities latent in the sailing ship, that the history of science is one of residue left behind as breakthrough follows breakthrough in a

---

[83] Joseph Owens, *An Interpretation of Existence* (Milwaukee: Bruce Publishing, 1968).

discontinuous fashion, that obsolescence rarely if ever occurs because the possibilities of a technology are fully achieved and hence exhausted, that obsolescence is the effect of a new technology only peripherally, if at all, "linked" with the old. To cite but one example: the flowering of sail did not occur in the heyday of the American clipper; it occurred in the early 20th century with the German Laeisz full-rigger, *Preussen*, and the five-masted barque, *Potosi*. These vessels were constructed long after sail was doomed as a commercial venture. Perhaps linotype is an exception, but, in general, technologies are simply cut down before they fully flower because a new technology emerges.

McLuhan/Nevitt speak of the divorce of "thinking" from "being" and of Greek Nature having been superimposed on the hidden ground of existence. The divorce, I do maintain, is already implicit in any act of reasoning whatsoever. Whereas the premises once set up within the mind truly do engender the conclusion formally (i.e., logically), thus permitting the mind to identify a major and minor through a middle term, the very setting up itself of the premises is a synthetic act which is reducible to neither premise taken in isolation not to both of them taken in isolation: A parallel line drawn through the apex is not contained analytically or implicitly within the definition of a triangle. Unless the mind synthesizes these two propositions, it will never conclude that the angles of a triangle are equal to two right angles. The integrating of the premises is not an act of definition. This act transcends the "meaning" that goes into it and is truly novel and creative. Without the act there simply is no meaning. Just why we do this nobody knows. But everybody over the age of discernment does it all the time.

Existentially, man causes the conclusion by making it be. This is the horse before the cart. The rearview mirror, the bright student seeing it all spread out for him, is the cart before the horse. The a priori for making sense is that sense be made. Meaning, nature, essence, concept, are all made to be by the activity of the mind itself. If existential activity—by existential activity I simply mean any "doing" at all; here the "doing" is mental doing—be considered a ground, then existence causes its own configuration. This configuration simultaneously emerges as a figure causing—in the formal and logical sense—its own proper ground within the intelligence and sensibility. This synthesis does put us on both sides of the Looking Glass. Everything is already done and over with, in neat sequential fashion, to the rearview mirror, to the bright student taking down notes. Everything is brand new and unexpected and creative to the doer. It would perhaps strain the normal use of language to call invention a "free" act; language is strained not at all to call this act nondeterministic, that is, not caused mechanically by any antecedents. Invention creates its own antecedents.[84]

And this moves me to comment on the McLuhan-Nevitt thesis that the West is blind to the effects of its own technologies. McLuhan, in private conversation and in correspondence, has suggested that the reason may lie in the division of life into public and private in the West and the absence of such a division in the East. The private man shuts himself away from the public consequences of his own technologies. He literally does not see them. Here I suggest a complementary cause gleaned from my own

---

[84] E.g., Arthur Koestler, *The Act of Creation* (New York: Macmillan, 1964); Frederick D. Wilhelmsen, "Reasoning and Computers," *Thought* 45: 179 (1970).

biases. If synthesizing premises transcends the formal structure of conclusions and indeed does cause these conclusions to exist, then no breakthrough or Eureka point can ever run ahead of itself and predict what will happen as a result of this or that scientific discovery. Synthesis—as within art, one of its highest manifestations—is never predictable, most especially to the man who is synthesizing. Creation is always blind. Existence is never grasped with the eye. Highly visual connectedness is the prerogative of those who sweep up behind the exhaust pipe of genius. Possibly for this reason scientists ought to have nothing to do with politics. Like God, they are too innocent.

Henry Ford I, horrified at the destruction of the rural America he loved, a destruction caused by his own motor car, recreated a miniscule figure of that old world in Greenfield Village in Dearborn, Michigan. Thomas Edison preached the Puritan ethic even as he threw absentmindedly into existence a new electronic ground which was to make that ethic impossible. And today Howard Hughes hides from his own empire behind an electronic screen that for a number of weeks made Hughes the most public absentee from the school of society in the world.

The authors speak of chiasmus—the slowdown of speedup, "visual perspective becomes an acoustic wraparound." Even the possibility of "seeing" the future though the rearview mirror by analytically deducing cultural effects from technological structures is today threatened because things happen so fast that they are pasts before they were futures. I am not so sanguine as are McLuhan/Nevitt about our now being able to "anticipate the effects . . . before allowing the causes to develop." We could make our own options, as the authors wish, only if political considerations governed scientific breakthrough. That situation does not exist as yet in the West. We are likely to miss the handrail as the merry-go-round speeds up. Electronic simultaneity is making the profession of futurist a pleasant *past*-time.

Electronic nowness, spoken of by McLuhan/Nevitt, causes antiquity. But it also abolishes the future as any significant dimension of the human spirit. The impossibility to predict future consequences of present acts is not only a mark of scientific absentmindedness. It is also a mark of the youth bred on television. This future blackout also suggests in a sinister fashion the new political assassin who murders under the electronic glare without any getaway car awaiting him in a darkened alley.[85] This may be a price we pay for the reintegration of sensorial experience after so many centuries of fragmentation, fragmentation united—let us never forget—with the ability to visualize future consequences.

The authors note that "concepts always follow percepts. In fact they are a kind of ossification of percepts." This kind of Lockeanism is the lapse one expects of Homers when they nod. I am inclined to affirm, on the contrary, that visual percepts have been mistaken for concepts ever since Descartes. The notes, of course, of this epistemological fallacy are as old as Plato's "Ideas." Percepts can be matched, for example, red on red, tone on tone. I can superimpose a cardboard triangle on another cardboard triangle. But I cannot superimpose or "match" (Platonic fashion) the concept of triangle with the concept of triangle. There are not two such concepts in the mind. I appeal here to the experience of the reader. Introspection reveals that the so-called convergence of triangles is the understanding of triangular meaning *in* triangular

---

[85] Jane Bret and Frederick D. Wilhelmsen, *Telepolitics: The Politics of Neuronic Man* (Montreal and New York: Tundra Books, 1972).

being grasped in some sensorial symbol, meaning in existence, not the other way around. Sharpness in insight is punchability, not thinkability. The authors take their enemies too seriously. There never was a clear and distinct idea. Blurred in and of themselves, concepts—"thinkability"—take on sharpness and precision only when used in judgments which affirm or deny existence. What is needed is the man of confused ideas and clear judgments. The man of clear ideas has the stare which suggests the sleepwalker. Judgment, like the reasoning composed of judgments, is a synthetic act. Both require a symbiosis of intelligence working through and in sensation. Meaning divorced from existence is Marcel's "The Fanaticized Consciousness."

Sensation itself is as creative as is reasoning and is as causal of its own effects. The scholastic *sensus communis* must not be taken as though it were an act which integrates fragmented information yielded by sight, sound, touch, etc. Sight, sound, touch, et al., are internal differentiations of an initially perceived sensorial whole. Children begin life wrapped within a sensorial whole that they subsequently differentiate. The rationalist divorce of sight from what McLuhan has often called "tactility" (not mere kinaesthesia but sensorial integration) wrought within the West that "disassociation of the sensibility" from the whole man commented on by T. S. Eliot. This divorce of sense from sense and of the spirit from matter caused the causal problem. Nobody has any problems about causality if he attends to his own experience. If he so does, he *knows* that he is the cause of what he does. But he cannot express this knowledge conceptually. He knows this, unless, of course, he has been shattered in fragments by the Humpty-Dumpty of the past few hundred years. I seem to remember that Humpty-Dumpty cannot be put back together again. Possibly those of us bred in an older order of things are all so shattered. Like Lady Bright, we shall come back the previous night.

Chapter Three

Formal Causality in Chesterton

Marshall McLuhan

One reason why Chesterton exasperated many fastidious souls relates to what I am going to illustrate as his concern with formal causality. He was vividly aware of his public and of its needs both to be cheered and to be straightened out. So pervasive is this feature in Chesterton that it scarcely matters at what page one opens in order to illustrate it. For example, the first page of his book on Dickens begins as follows:

> Much of our modern difficulty, in religion and other things, arises merely from this: that we confuse the word "indefinable" with the word "vague." If someone speaks of a spiritual fact as "indefinable" we promptly picture something misty, a cloud with indeterminate edges. But this is an error even in commonplace logic. The thing that cannot be defined is the first thing; the primary

> fact. It is our arms and legs, our pots and pans, that are indefinable.[86]

Here Chesterton is quite aware that the problems of his time are not without a strong affinity for each other. If one looks at the opening objections in the Thomistic article, one finds a similar awareness of likeness in diversity. Aquinas always put his public on view at the opening of his disputed questions, and Chesterton usually gives strong indications of the kinds of people and the kinds of problems with which he is dealing. On the second page of the same book on Dickens, he focuses this larger awareness of audience on Dickens itself:

> In everyday talk, or in any of our journals, we may find the loose but important phrase, "Why have we no great men today? Why have we no great men like Thackeray, or Carlyle, or Dickens?" Do not let us dismiss this expression, because it appears loose or arbitrary. "Great" does mean something, and the test of its actuality is to be found by noting how instinctively and incisively we do apply it to some men and not to others; above all how instinctively and incisively we do apply it to four or five men in the Victorian era, four or five men of whom Dickens was not the least. The term is found to fit a definite thing. Dickens was what it means.[87]

Joseph Conrad, addressing his public, said: "My task . . . is before all, to make you *see*."[88] He was drawing attention to a defect in his readers, a defect

---

[86] G. K. Chesterton, *Dickens* (London: Methuen, 1906): 1.
[87] Ibid.: 2.
[88] Joseph Conrad, "Preface" to *The Nigger of the 'Narcissus'* (London: Gresham Publishing Company, 1925): x.

which he was concerned to supply and to repair. This, in turn, is to draw attention to the public as a formal cause in the sense that the public is in need of some help in some area of concern, an area in which it is ignorant, or mistaken, or confused. Ezra Pound devoted much of his work to the theme that the artist's work is to *make it new*. In this respect it is possible to point out that the formal cause, or the public itself, is in perpetual flux and always in need of clarification and re-focusing of its problems. Style itself, whether in poetry or painting or music, is a way of seeing and knowing, which is otherwise unobtainable. In his book, *The Problem of Style*, Middleton Murry pointed out "style is a way of seeing." To mention this work is to remind ourselves of the much greater work of Rémy de Gourmont, *Le Problème du Style*. The style is the response of the artist to his audience and its needs. Chesterton's style was playful in an age that was very earnest, and his perceptions and thoughts were paradoxical or multifaceted in a time that was full of intense specialism in politics and economics and religion.

Earlier I had mentioned that Aquinas put his public in full view of his readers at the beginning of each article. His public is that which shapes and patterns his discourse and takes the form of an inventory of objections which cover the whole spectrum of the confusions and inadequacies of his contemporaries. The very first objection, at the very beginning of the *Summa*, notes: "It seems that, beside the philosophical sciences, we have no need of any further knowledge. For man should not seek to know what is above reason. '*Seek not the things that are too high for thee.*' (Ecclus. III:22)"

The answers to the objections pursue the confusions of his readers more closely still. It appears that no Thomist has considered the audience or public of a philosopher as the formal cause of his work. Yet this is truly the case in Plato and Aristotle as well as in Aquinas. If the formal cause of the Incarnation is fallen man, it is not surprising that the misguided audience of the creative person should be the formal cause of his endeavours.

Perhaps, before moving on, I should pause to indicate why Western philosophers and scholars may have shirked consideration of formal causality in the study of the arts and sciences. Since scarcely anybody has studied the audience of any writer from Plato to the present, there must surely be both a profound and a simple reason for so vast and consistent an omission. I suggest that this reason is to be found in the visual bias of Western man. Visual man is typically concerned with the lineal and the connected and the logical. Visual order has regard to *figure* and not to *ground*. The audience is always the hidden *ground* rather than the *figure* of any discourse. The *ground* is discontinuous, murky and dynamic, whereas the *figure* tends to be clear and distinct and static. However, without the interplay of *figure* and *ground*, no art or knowledge is possible. It might even be argued that the abrupt and bumpy and grotesquely sprockety contours of Chesterton's prose are very much a response of his sensitivity to a perverse and misbegotten public that he earnestly but good-naturedly was determined to redeem from its banalities.

Arthur Miller recently wrote a remarkable essay about his own public and its role in creating drama.[89] 1949 was the eve of network TV when a totally new public came into play. Up until then, there had been a

---

89 Arthur Miller, "1949: The Year It Came Apart," *New York Magazine* 30 Dec. 1974.

kind of homogeneous audience from New York to San Francisco:

> In many ways it was a good audience, but the important point to remember is that it was the only one, and therefore catholic. Traditionally it could applaud the Ziegfeld Follies one night and O'Neill the next, and if it never made great hits of Odets's plays, it affected to regard him as the white-haired boy. Both O'Neill and Odets would privately decry the audience as Philistine and pampered, but it was the audience they set about to save from its triviality, for they could not really conceive there could be another.[90]

In the everyday order, formal causality reveals itself by its *effects*. There is a strange paradox in this, because since the effects come from the hidden *ground* of situations, the effects usually appear before their causes. When a Darwin or an Einstein appears, we say "the time was ripe" and that the *figure* appeared in its natural *ground*. Chesterton was almost oriental in his sensitivity to effects, his capacity for noting the consequences embedded in innovations and special attitudes or situations. In fact, Chesterton was always aware of "the law of the situation." This phrase was much used by Mary Parker Follett, the inventor of modern management studies. She was always concerned with discovering the question rather than the answer. It was she who began to ask managers: "What business do you think you are in?" They would point to the *figure* in their enterprise and she would give the *ground*, or the *effects* of the *figure*. She would point out to a windowblind manufacturer that he was really in the business of environmental light control.

---

90 Ibid.

With this knowledge, the manufacturer is not likely to be disconcerted by an innovation like the invention of Venetian blinds.

In *Tremendous Trifles*, Chesterton observes:

> You cannot see a wind; you can only see that there is a wind. So, also, you cannot see a revolution; you can only see that there is a revolution. And there never has been in the history of the world a real revolution, brutally active and decisive, which was not preceded by unrest and new dogma in the reign of invisible things. All revolutions began by being abstract. Most revolutions began by being quite pedantically abstract.
>
> The wind is up above the world before a twig on the tree has moved. So there must always be a battle in the sky before there is a battle on the earth.[91]

Chesterton's awareness of the *figure/ground* consequences pervades his studies of history and human thought in general. It made it easy for him to enter the field of detective fiction, since the detective story is written backwards, starting with the effects, and discovering the cause later, and, as it were, incidentally. The history of detective fiction, at least since Edgar Poe, relates to the law of the situation very intimately.

Poe is perhaps best known for his account of the composition of "The Raven." He explained that, seeking in the first place to achieve an effect of

---

[91] G. K. Chesterton, *Tremendous Trifles* (New York: Dodd, Mead, 1909): 91.

maximal melancholy and gloom, he set about discovering the means to get this effect, noting that art must always start with the *effect.* This is another way of saying that art must start with formal cause, and with concern with the audience. Sherlock Holmes frequently explained to Watson (who was typical of the unenlightened public) that the detective must put himself in the place of the criminal. The criminal is the person who is entirely concerned with *effects.* He considers the entire situation as one to be manipulated, both *figure* and *ground*, in order to achieve a very special effect. The criminal, like the artist, takes into account both the *figure* and the *ground*, that is, the work to be done in order that the effect may be achieved. It is this interplay between *figure* and *ground*, and the confronting of the latter in the situation, which gives to the detective story so much of the poetic character. Chesterton's *Father Brown* is always sensitive to the hidden laws of the situation that are so easily obscured by the ordinary concern with *figure* and points of view: for it is of the essence of formal causality that it is not a point of view, but, rather, a statement of a situation. In "The Queer Feet," Father Brown says:

> "A crime," he said slowly, "is like any other work of art. Don't look surprised; crimes are by no means the only works of art that come from an infernal workshop. But every work of art, divine or diabolic, has one indispensable mark—I mean, that the centre of it is simple, however much the fulfilment may be complicated."[92]

---

[92] G. K. Chesterton, "The Queer Feet," *The Father Brown Stories* (London: Cassell, 1966): 51.

He continues:

> But every clever crime is founded ultimately on some one quite simple fact—some fact that is not itself mysterious. The mystification comes in covering it up, in leading men's thoughts away from it. This large and subtle and (in the ordinary course) most profitable crime, was built on the plain fact that a gentleman's evening dress is the same as a waiter's. All the rest was acting, and thundering good acting, too.[93]

The covering-up process is done by simply introducing points of view. Points of view are inevitably alien to the law of the situation, and especially alien to formal causality. Points of view are always reserved for the police and the slow-witted. In the world of Sherlock Holmes and much detective fiction, the rational point of view, with its plodding accumulation of evidence, is reserved for Lestrade and the police in general.

Formal causality is not something that can be abstracted, since it is always a dynamic relation between the user and the ever-changing situation. Cardinal Newman recognised this *in An Essay on the Development of Christian Doctrine*:

> Moreover, an idea not only modifies but is modified, or at least influenced, by the state of things in which it is carried out, and is dependent in various ways on the circumstances which surround it. Its development proceeds quickly or slowly, as it may be; the order of succession in its various stages is variable; it shows differently in a small

---

[93] Ibid.: 52.

> sphere of action and in an extended; it may be interrupted, retarded, mutilated, distorted by external violence; it may be enfeebled by the effort of ridding itself of domestic foes; it may be impeded and swayed or even absorbed by counter energetic ideas; it may be coloured by the received tone of thought into which it comes, or depraved by the intrusion of foreign principles, or at length shattered by the development of some original fault within it.[94]

It was the "rhetorical" interplay between philosophy and its public which was eliminated by Descartes in the seventeenth century with the result that formal cause was transferred from the public to the subjective life of the individual philosopher or student of philosophy. The further consequence was that the "content" of philosophy and the arts became relegated to efficient causality. Formal causality simply ceased to have any *conscious* role in the arts and sciences from then until our own day. Chesterton was part of the *avant-garde* in re-discovering formal causality in his multi-levelled grasp of his public and his themes.

---

[94] John Henry Cardinal Newman, *An Essay on the Development of Christian Doctrine* (New York: Doubleday, 1960): 62.

Chapter Four

On Formal Cause

Eric McLuhan

Preamble

The Four Cowses (tetra bukolos aitia—execrable Greek, I know...)
Of course, you realize that McLuhan's work was all in the area of Formal Cause. I mean Farm'l Cows, as a murder of corpse.

There are the Four Cowses, as you know.

There is Efficient Cows, Material Cows and Final Cows, in addition to Farm'l Cows. Of the four, Farm'l Cows is the fundamental one and it contains all of the udders. It is the one that really concerns effects, namely side-effects.

All of the other "effects" (the ones Science and Sociology are ga-ga about) are part of Efficient Cows, which is the only one that works sequentially. (So one Cows can cause another Cows, which . . . etc.) Efficient Cows is also the area where people love to wax moralistic, and provides a big distraction from the real action (you know where). And EC is also the area where most people who imagine they are studying communication spend all of their time. Efficient is also concerned with efficiency and waste and the morals of it all. Enough to cow one.

Material Cows concerns the material that makes up something, the bricks, steel, paper, etc. Efficient Cows concerns the maker and the making/assembling process (which the communists specialize in, putting all their stress on ownership of the means of production etc.).

Final Cows is the thing, considered in itself. Nobody these days gets very excited about Final Cows. But Farm'l Cows, ah! There is moostery and excitement galore. VERY few people understand Farm'l Cows: it embraces all of what we call media and culture...

—I wrote this piece about cowsality for a McLuhan devotee called "Cattle Ken." His name was the spur. EM

On Formal Cause

McLuhan: Harold Innis was one of the very few people since Plato to show serious interest in formal causes and the effects that result from the formal structure of total situations.

—from the interview of Marshall McLuhan by Hubert Hoskins, entitled *Electric Consciousness and the Church.*

HH: "....so what really counts is not what but how?"
McLuhan: "yes"

—Ibid.

...People do not want to know the cause of anything. They do not want to know why radio caused Hitler and Ghandi alike. They do not want to know that print caused anything whatever. As users of these media, they wish merely to get inside, hoping perhaps to add another layer to their environment in the manner of "The Chambered Nautilus" of Oliver Wendell Holmes.

The total non-response of hundreds of thousands of people to the suggestion that there was an actual physical environmental, man-made cause of drug addiction in our time startled me into study of the attitude of the scientific community to causation. It does not take long to discover that all of the sciences, physical and social, are interested only in describing and measuring effects while ignoring causation entirely. A connection is not a cause but a hang-up. This is not a matter that can be properly discussed in this [head]note, but the absence of interest in causation cannot persist in the new age of ecology. Ecology does not seek connections, but patterns. It does not seek quantities, but satisfactions and understanding. The pioneer work of Harold Innis in the study of causality relating to the material media of communication had no followers, despite his being surrounded with academic admirers. The student of media will discover that for the past 500 years Western Science has systematically excluded the study of causation by the simple process of fragmentation and quantification.[95]

95 The concluding paragraphs of Marshall McLuhan's essay, 'Education in the Electronic Age"—The text of an address to the Provincial Committee on the Aims and Objectives of Education of the Schools of Ontario, on January 19, 1967. Printed as Chapter 12.3 in H. A. Stevenson, R. M. Stamp, and J. D. Wilson eds. *The Best of Times/The Worst of Times: Contemporary Issues in Canadian Education* (Toronto and Montreal: Holt, Rinehart and Winston of Canada Limited, 1972): 530-531.

Formal causality kicks in whenever "coming events cast their shadows before them." Formal cause is still, in our time, hugely mysterious: The literate mind finds it is too paradoxical and irrational. It deals with environmental processes and it works outside of time. The effects—those long shadows—arrive first; the causes take a while longer.[96] Most of the effects of any medium or innovation occur before the arrival of the innovation itself. A vortex of these effects tends, in time, to become the innovation. A few examples of formal cause at work will serve to illustrate the matter. David Hockney's recent study, *Secret Knowledge*, details how Flemish and other artists of the early 15th century literally paved the way for the Gutenberg press a decade or so later with their optical experiments.[97] Their lenses and mirrors enabled them to explore in depth as never before precision of point of view, perspective, and chiaroscuro, greatly intensifying the visual stress they could bring to bear in their paintings, and paving the way for the press. First come the effects.

George Steiner discusses how formal cause operates dramatically at the heart of Greek tragedy:

> We *know* what will happen to Agamemnon when he enters the house, each instant of the

---

[96] Perhaps this is what Aristotle had in mind when he remarked, about thinking and perceiving, that "the exercise of their functions comes before the faculties themselves." *Aristotle: On the Soul, Parva Naturalia, On Breath*, trans. W. S. Hett (Cambridge, MA: Harvard University Press/London: W. Heinemann, 1957): 84, 85 (II.4.19-20): proteron gar eisi ton dynameon ai energeiai kai ai praxeis kata ton logon: πρότερον γάρ εἰσι τῶν δυνάμεων αἱ ἐνέργειαι καὶ αἱ πράξεις κατὰ τὸν λόγον.

[97] David Hockney, *Secret Knowledge: Discovering the Lost Techniques of the Old Masters* (London: Thames and Hudson, 2001).

> *agon* has been announced and prepared for. We know precisely what Oedipus will discover—in a crucial sense he too has known all along. Yet with each narration or performance of the fable our sense of shock is renewed. The tragic vision of Greek literature turns on this deep paradox: the event most expected, most consequent on the internal logic of action, is also the most surprising.[98]

Jane Jacobs approaches cities structurally, using formal cause. As she reminds us, the dogma of agricultural primacy says, "agriculture first, cities later."

> Current theory in many fields—economics, history, anthropology—assumes that cities are built upon a rural economic base. If my observations and reasoning are correct, the reverse is true: that is, rural economies, including agricultural work, are directly built upon city economies and city work.[99]

Common sense and efficient cause naturally suggest the city grows slowly out of the countryside. But formal cause reveals that a vortex of effects comes first:

> Rural production is literally the creation of city consumption.. That is to say, city economies invent the things that are to become city imports from the rural world, and then they reinvent the rural world so it can supply those imports. This, as far as I can see, is the only

[98] *After Babel* (London, New York, Toronto: Oxford University Press, 1975): 149.

[99] *The Economy of Cities* (New York: Random House, 1969): 1-2.

> way in which rural economies develop at all, agricultural primacy notwithstanding.[100]

T. S. Eliot would identify this same pattern of conformity between a *figure* and its *ground* as defining a tradition and an individual talent. In the electric age we can easily see that the vortex of effects of any innovation always precedes its causes. So, for example, if we see on every hand the effects of antigravity in the form of airplanes and spacecraft and submarines, then it is easy to predict that actual antigravity will soon be a feature of everyday life. And the same might be said of telepathy, since we have everywhere around us the effects of it in the form of radio, telephones, wireless computing, etc.

As far as I know, Aristotle, the first to write about formal cause, never quite states right out that the formal cause of something is the *ground* that gives rise to it, though he tries to do so on many occasions. Here is the conventional view of Aristotle's system of causes:

> The production of works of art, to which Aristotle himself frequently turns for examples, most readily illustrates these four different kinds of causes. In making a shoe, the material cause is that out of which the shoe is made—the leather or hide. The efficient cause is the

---

[100] Ibid.: 38. The operation of formal cause is clearly evident in detective stories, where the detective is presented first with the effects and has to use formal cause to work backwards to the (efficient) cause of the crime. My father, who loved detective stories, noted in pencil on the front flyleaf of one such paperback novel that Watson was the formal cause of Holmes as Jeeves was of Bertie Wooster. (*The Seven-Per-Cent Solution: Being a Reprint from the Reminiscences of John H. Watson, M.D., as edited by Nicholas Meyer.* New York: Ballantine Books, 1974, 1975.)

shoemaker, or more precisely the shoemaker's acts that transform the raw material into the finished product. The formal cause is the pattern which directs the work; it is, in a sense, the definition or type of the thing to be made, which, beginning as a plan in the artist's mind, appears at the end of the work in the transformed material as its own intrinsic form. The protection of the foot is the final cause or end—that for the sake of which the shoe was made.

Two of the four causes seem to be less discernible in nature than in art. The material and efficient causes remain evident enough. The material cause can usually be identified as that which undergoes the change—the thing which grows, alters in color, or moves from place to place. The efficient cause is always that by which the change is produced. It is the moving cause working on that which is susceptible to change, e.g., the fire heating the water, the rolling stone setting another stone in motion.

But the formal cause is not as apparent in nature as in art. Whereas in art it can be identified by reference to the plan in the maker's mind, it must be discovered in nature in the change itself, as that which completes the process. For example the redness which the apple takes on in ripening is the formal cause of its alteration in color. The trouble with the final cause is that it so often tends to be inseparable from the formal cause; for unless some extrinsic purpose can be found for a natural change—some end beyond itself which the change serves—the final cause, or that for the sake of which the change took place, is no other than the quality or form which the matter assumes as a result of its transformation.[101]

Aristotle's four causes make up nature. As Frederick Wilhelmsen points out, "often philosophers speak of Aristotle's causes as though they operated *on* or *within* nature. This is not quite accurate. Nature and the four causes are one. *Reality is causality.* These causes compose ... what this author calls 'the analytic of ... being'."[102] Formal cause is the *ground* for the material, efficient and final causes; in that sense, it "contains all the other causes." *Simile modo,* the Literal Sense contains the other Senses. (See *Laws of Media*[103] (Chapter 5) for other parallels to these "fours.") Aristotle points out the blindness conferred by taking a moral approach (good or bad opinion) to matters of formal awareness and knowing: "it is impossible to have opinion and knowledge at the same time about the same object..." (οὐδέ δοξάζειν ἅμα τὸ αὐτὸ καὶ ἐπίστασθαι ἐνδέχεται).[104] In any field, analysis via the moral approach means specializing in the Moral Level of interpretation. Moralism works at the same level as efficient cause; both tend to become preoccupations and strong biases.[105] Often, the

---

[101] *Great Books of the Western World,* ed. R. M. Hutchins. Volume Two (the first half of the *Syntopicon*), *The Great Ideas: I,* ed. Mortimer Adler (Chicago: University of Chicago Press/ Encyclopædia Britannica, 1952): 156.

[102] Frederick D. Wilhelmsen, *The Paradoxical Structure of Existence* (Irving, TX: University of Dallas Press, 1970): 22.

[103] Marshall McLuhan and Eric McLuhan, *Laws of Media: The New Science* (Toronto: University of Toronto Press, 1988).

[104] *Aristotle: Posterior Analytics,* trans., Hugh Tredennick; bound with *Topica,* trans., E. S. Forster. (London: William Heinemann/ Cambridge, MA: Harvard University Press, Loeb Classical Library, 1960), Book I, Ch. Xxxiii.89a (end): 170, 171.

[105] A propos the moral outlook, McLuhan remarked,

moralist approach is used as a way to evade a difficult task such as studying the object of the denouncement. This is certainly true of media study, where people will wax moralistic over the content and its effects as a means of ignoring the medium itself.

> Don't ask me if this is a good thing. I don't feel that any person is able yet to make value judgments of that sort. Our job is diagnosis and observation prior to judgment. But I have noticed over and over again that when people ask in the middle of some effort to chart an actual development, "Is this a good thing?" they always mean, "Is this a good thing for me?" "How does it affect me? - I'm a doctor." Or "How will it affect me? - I'm an architect." They don't mean, "Is it good?" They mean, "What will it do to me?" It took me years to find out what they really meant by this strange constant request for value judgment. It's a Protestant sort of fixation, this "Is it a good or a bad thing?" It comes from an obsession with efficient causes at an applied moment. The actual obsession with efficient causality—what you call activism—is basic to the Protestant outlook."

--From a transcript of an informal address, given at the 12th annual seminarians' Conference, St. Michael's College, University of Toronto, 29-31 August 1959, and published in the volume, *Communications and the Word of God*, by St. Michael's College, pp. 9-22. Rpt., *The Medium and the Light* (Toronto: Stoddart, 1999): 37. In a letter to the editor of *Commonweal* about their review (issue of May 25, 1979) of Elizabeth Eisenstein's study, he wrote:

> [My book] *The Gutenberg Galaxy* makes no personal value judgments because it is concerned with *formal* causality and the study of effects, with reception aesthetics. Professor Eisenstein is concerned with *efficient* causality: her title is *The Printing Press as an Agent of Change*! This level of descriptive narrative leaves ample room for the noting of *content* and the making of value judgments, both of which are alien to the level of formal causality.
>
> "In a utilitarian society, untrained in the formal structures and patterns of effect, efficient causality and moralizing is the only acceptable norm. Having written *The Gutenberg Galaxy* by way of turning in a fire alarm, it is curious to find some readers have charged me with arson..."

Stephen Hawking found the same thing with reference to his work, much of which concerns formal causes:

> My approach has been described as naïve and simpleminded. I have been variously called a nominalist, an instrumentalist, a positivist, a realist, and several other ists. The technique seems to be refutation by denigration: If you can attach a label to my approach, you don't have to say what is wrong with it. Surely everyone knows the fatal errors of all those isms.[106]

When Stephen Hawking discusses his own theory of communication, it becomes immediately obvious that he works constantly with formal cause. One function of a scientific theory is to probe reality, to prod it into revealing itself: "we cannot distinguish what is real about the universe without a theory." A good, elegant theory will accomplish certain tasks in the area of efficient cause, such as describing a wide array of observations and predicting the results of new ones. "Beyond that, it makes no sense, "he points out, "to ask if [a theory] corresponds to reality, because we do not know what reality is independent of a theory.[107] A scientific theory is a way of seeing, and as such a formal cause of reality.

Adolf Hildebrand asserted that the formal cause of a work of art was realized as an effect of the item. In

---

[106] Stephen Hawking, *Black Holes and Baby Universes and Other Essays* (New York, London, Toronto, Sydney, Auckland: Bantam Books, 1993): 43. He adds, "The person who called me a positivist went on to add that everyone knew that positivism was out of date—another case of refutation by denigration." (44). McLuhan has enjoyed precisely the same sort of attention from his critics and from academic experts alike.

[107] Ibid.: 44

his study of *The Problem of Form in Painting and Sculpture*,[108] he wrote, "in true Art the actual form has its reality only as an effect."[109] That is, the form occurs outside the painting or piece of sculpture, and as a result of its interaction with an audience. The same rules apply to poetry and the other arts. Writing about metrics, Paul Fussell observed,

> To do something to the reader is the end of poetry: a poem is less a notation on a page or a sequence of uttered sounds than a shaped and measured formal effect that impinges upon a reader or hearer. The reality of the poem is in its impingement... The poet whose metrical effects actually work upon a reader reveals that he has attained an understanding of what man in general is like.[110]

Hildebrand distinguished two kinds of form, perceptual and actual. Perceptual form is how the thing appears or strikes the imagination, and it may vary with point of view, lighting, etc. Actual form is, he says, "inferred from the appearance."[111] Like formal cause, Hildebrand's actual form is an active force, not a passive pattern or container. The two kinds of form are rather close to what we used to call "structural impact" and "sensory closure." Both are structural, and neither inheres in the object or *figure*.

---

108 Second edition, translated and revised with the author's co-operation by Max Meyer and Robert Morris Ogden (New York: G. E. Stechert & Co., 1932).
109 Ibid.: 45.
110 Paul Fussell, Jr., *Poetic Meter and Poetic Form* (New York: Random House, 1965): 110.
111 Hildebrand, *Op. Cit.*: 36.

With formal cause, Aristotle updates the Ancients' notion of logos

Aristotle frequently discusses formal causality in the *Metaphysics*. In Book I Ch. 6, he makes a remarkable observation concerning Plato's relation to the Pythagoreans: In thinkers before Plato, he avers, there is to be found "no tincture of Dialectic." Aristotle offers this comment to explain why Plato chose to base the Forms in the region of his grammatical inquiries involving etymology and definitions.

> His divergence from the Pythagoreans in making the One and the Numbers separate from things, and his introduction of the Forms, were due to his inquiries in the region of definitions (for the earlier thinkers had no tincture of dialectic), and his making the other entity ... *etc.*[112]

The word Aristotle uses for "forms" is *eidon*, and the word that is translated into English as "definitions" is *logois*:

> καὶ ἡ τῶν ειδῶν εἰσαγωγὴ διὰ τὴν έν τοῖσ λόγοισ ἐγένετο οκέψιν (οἱ γὰρ πρότεροι διαλεκτικῆσ οὐ μετεῖχον)

[112] *Metaphysics*, I.6.30 (987b). The translation is by W. D. Ross; it agrees exactly with McKeon's.

Aristotle consistently equates form and definition, and definition and the *logos* of a thing.[113] He cites the antiquity of the notion as extending back at least to Empedocles:

> ...for a thing's "nature" is much more a first principle (or "Cause") than it is matter. (Indeed, in some places even Empedocles, being led and guided by Truth herself, stumbles upon this, and is forced to assert that it is the *logos* which is a thing's essence or nature ....)
>
> ἀρχὴ γὰρ ἡ φύσισ μαλλον τῆσ ὕλησ. (ἐνιαχοῦ δέ που αὐτῇ καὶ Ἐμπεδοκλῆσ περιπίπτει ἀγόμενοσ ὑπ' αὐτῆσ τῆσ ἀληθεΐασ, καὶ τὴν οὐσίαν καὶ τὴν θύσιν ἀναγκάζεται θάναι τὸν λόγον εἶναι, οἷον ὀστοῦν ἀποδιδοὺσ τί ἐστιν.[114]

Definition and *logos* share another process, one that springs from the old idea of *logos* as "transforming word."

To the ancient understanding, the *logos* was charged with the power to bring things into being. The gods themselves spoke in thunder, and their speech could—and frequently did—alter the world and influence the course of events. Naming a thing, tantamount to defining it, meant giving it a structure and an existence. The name—*logos*—was the thing's

---

113 Let us not casually assume that he means what we do by "definition." He is thinking in Greek; we, in Latin and English. *De-finite*, means being sensitive to the boundaries of the thing, the edge that circumscribes things finite. Observing the *figure/ground interface* between it and non-finitude. Where does it depart from or o'erleap finitude?

114 Aristotle, *Parts of Animals*, Book I, Ch. 1, 18-22 (642a.18-22). (London: William Heinemann/Cambridge, MA: Harvard University Press, Loeb Classical Library, 1937): 76-77.

pattern of being, its essence, its definition. In the process of choosing and uttering a thing's name, the thing itself was called into existence.[115] Naming and giving something definition was rather more than application of arbitrary labels. The name more than simply *meant* the thing, and vice-versa: the two were so closely interrelated as to be one. Name and thing embody each other. Defining and naming were each *constitutive* acts; they were equivalent: this active *logos* appears in *Genesis* as God creates the universe by means of speech. God utters the universe at the creation, by speaking its name. He, as it were, calls the universe out of non-being into being.[116] Every human act of naming echoes this act of knowing and making. A kind of replay or re-cognition, human naming demands precise perceptual knowledge of the thing and parodies the Divine act of naming and making. Here is *le mot juste* with a vengeance. So the ancients ever regarded etymology and the study of names as high science. It could provide a direct route to knowing the essential nature of things—exactly the domain of formal causality.[117] Finding the etymology

---

115 Each time the womb "speaks," the utterance is a child. At the birth, the native midwife stands nearby the mother and calls out various names until the child, hearing its name, decides to be born.

116 So, Gilson remarks, echoing Aquinas, "God *knows* essences, but He *says* existences, and He does not say all that He knows." Etienne Gilson, *Being and Some Philosophers* (Toronto: Pontifical Institute of Mediæval Studies, 1949, Rev., 1952): 169.

117 In modern science, the theory has the same effect as the name. Stephen Hawking observes that "it makes no sense to ask if [a theory] corresponds to reality, because we do not know what reality is independent of a theory... It is no good appealing to reality because we don't have a model independent concept of reality.... The unspoken belief in a model independent reality is the underlying reason for the difficulties philosophers of science have with quantum mechanics and the uncertainty principle." Hawking, *Op. Cit.*: 44-45.

meant peeling back layer after layer of concepts to expose the original perceptual configuration, where the true nature of the thing is recorded.

Formal cause unites mode of being and entelechy or constituent pattern

With these matters in mind, view Aristotle's assertion, opening the *Poetics*, that "*Mimesis* is the process by which all men learn," and, in *De Anima*, the celebrated passage,

> ... the soul is in a way all existing things... Within the soul, the faculties of knowledge and sensation are potentially these objects ... They must be either the things themselves or their forms. The former alternative is of course impossible: it is not the stone which is present in the soul but its form.
>
> It follows that the soul is analogous to the hand; for as the hand is a tool of tools, so the mind is the form of forms and sense the form of sensible things.[118]

> Oti he psyche ta ontai tos esti panta... he men dynamei eis ta dynamei, he d' entelecheia eis ta entelecheia. Tes de psyches to aisthetikon kai ta epistemonikon dynamei tauta esti, to men

[118] McKeon's translation: opening of *De Anima*, Book III, Chapter 8; 431`b20-432a.

> episteton to de aistheton. Anagke d' he auta he ta eide einai. Auta men gar de ou. Ou gar ho lithos en te psyche, alla to eidos. Oste he psyche hosper he cheir estin. Kai gar he cheir organon estin organon, kai nous eidos eidon kai he eisthesis eidos aistheton.

> ὅτι ἡ ψυχὴ τὰ ὄντα πώς ἐστι πάντα...ἡ μὲν δυνάμει εἰς τὰ δυνάμει, ἡ δ' ἐντελεχείᾳ εἰς τὰ ἐντελεχείᾳ· τῆς δὲ ψυχῆς τὸ αἰσθητικὸν καὶ τὸ ἐπιστημονικὸν δυνάμει ταὐτά ἐστι, τὸ μὲν <τὸ> ἐπιστητὸν τὸ δὲ <τὸ> αἰσθητόν. ἀνάγκη δ' ἢ αὐτὰ ἢ τὰ εἴδη εἶναι. αὐτὰ μὲν δὴ οὔ· οὐ γὰρ ὁ λίθος ἐν τῇ ψυχῇ, ἀλλὰ τὸ εἶδος· ὥστε ἡ ψυχὴ ὥσπερ ἡ χείρ ἐστιν· καὶ γὰρ ἡ χεὶρ ὄργανόν ἐστιν ὀργάνων, καὶ ὁ νοῦς εἶδος εἰδῶν καὶ ἡ αἴσθησις εἶδος αἰσθητῶν.[119]

In the dialogue named for Cratylus, the follower of Heraclitus, Plato has this apposite exchange between Socrates and Cratylus:

> **Socrates**: But if these things are only to be known through names, how can we suppose that the givers of names had knowledge, or were legislators before there were names at all, and therefore before they could have known them?
>
> **Cratylus**: I believe, Socrates, the true account of the matter to be, that a power more than human gave things their first names, and that the names which were

---

[119] Loeb: 178-180. Keep this in mind in the discussion below: For Aristotle, *nous* and *aisthesis* are both *eide*.

> thus given are necessarily their true names.[120]

Marshall McLuhan comments:

> Obviously, with this kind of importance associated with the names of things, and of gods, heroes, and legendary beings, etymology would be a main source of scientific and moral enlightenment. And such was the case. The prolific labors of the etymologists reflected in Plato's *Cratylus*, but begun centuries before and continued until the seventeenth century, are as much the concern of the historian of philosophy and of science as of the historian of letters and culture. Indeed, it was not only in antiquity but until the Cartesian revolution that language was viewed as simultaneously linking and harmonizing all the intellectual and physical functions of man and of the physical world as well.
>
> At any time from Plato to Francis Bacon the statement of Cratylus would have made sense, and would have evoked respect even when its wider implications were rejected. With the opening of the Christian era, the doctrine of Cratylus gained new significance from scriptural exegesis, and especially from Genesis 2.19:
>
> > And out of the ground the Lord God formed every beast of the field, and every fowl of the air; and brought them unto the man to see what he would call them:

---

[120] Jowett (New York, 1895): I, 678.

> and whatsoever he called every living creature, that was the name thereof.

McLuhan remarks further:

> The doctrine of names is, of course, the doctrine of essence and not a naïve notion of oral terminology. The scriptural exegetists will hold, as Francis Bacon held, that Adam possessed metaphysical knowledge in a very high degree. To him the whole of nature was a book which he could read with ease. He lost his ability to read this language as a result of his fall; and Solomon alone of the sons of men has ever recovered the power to read the book of nature. The business of art is, however, to recover the knowledge of that language which once man held by nature. The problem as to which of the arts should have priority in the work of explaining man and nature had arisen among the pre-Socratic philosophers. Grammar, or allegorical exegesis of natural phenomena, as well as of folk myths and even the works of Homer and Hesiod, enjoyed many advantages for the task. In the *Cratylus*, however, Plato asserts the superior claims of dialectics for the same work, but, as a philosopher who habitually employed the grammatical modes of poetry and myth to express his own most significant and esoteric teaching, he is far from confident that grammar can be or ought to be entirely superseded. Shortly afterwards, however, Aristotle

established the nature of non-grammatical scientific method in the *Posterior Analytics.*[121]

In Book V of the *Metaphysics,* Aristotle again introduces all four causes, as though for the first time:

> "Cause" means (1) that from which, as immanent material, a thing comes into being, e.g. the bronze is the cause of the statue and the silver of the saucer, and so are the classes which include these. (2) the form or pattern, i.e. the definition of the essence, and the classes which include this (e.g. the ratio 2:1 and number in general are causes of the octave), and the parts included in the definition. (3) That from which the change or the resting from change first begins; e.g. the adviser is a cause of the action, and the father a cause of the child, and in general the maker a cause of the thing made and the change-producing of the changing. (4) The end, i.e. that for the sake of which a thing is...[122]

Or in other words,

> αἴτιον λέγεται ἕνα μὲν τρόπον ἐξ οὗ γίγνεταί τι ἐνυπάρχοντοσ, οἷον ὁ χαλκὸσ τοῦ ἀνδριάντοσ καὶ ὁ ἄργυροσ τῆσ φιάλησ καὶ τὰ τούτων γένη: ἄλλον δὲ τὸ εἶδοσ και τὸ παράδειγμα, τοῦτο δ' ἐστὶν ὁ λόγοσ τοῦ τί ἦν εἶναι καὶ τὰ τούτου γένη (οἷον τοῦ διὰ πασῶν τὸ δύο πρὸσ ἓν καὶ ὅλωσ ὁ ἀριθμόσ) καὶ τὰ μέρη τὰ ἐν τῷ λόγῳ. ἔτι ὅθεν ἡ ἀρχὴ τῆσ

---

[121] Marshall McLuhan, *The Classical Trivium: The Place of Thomas Nashe in the Learning of his Time* (Corte Madera, CA: Gingko Press, 2006): 16-17.

[122] *Metaphysics*, V.2.25, 30 (1013a).

> μεταβολῆσ ἡ πρώτη ἢ τῆσ ἠρεμήσεωσ, οἷον ὁ Βουλεύσασ αἴτιοσ, καὶ ὁ πατὴρ τοῦ τέκνου καὶ ὅλωσ τὸ ποιοῦν τοῦ ποιουμένου καὶ τὸ μεταβλητικὸν τοῦ μεταβάλλοντοξ. ἔτι ὡσ τὸ τέλοσ: τοῦτο δ' ἐστι τὸ οὗ ἕνεκα...

Once again, he uses *aitia* for cause in general,[123] and *eidos* for form (formal cause)—and *logos* is twice translated as "definition." The form or pattern of the thing is the *logos* of its essence. Somewhat earlier, in the first Book, Aristotle had drawn together formal cause, and *logos* ("definition") and essence (the translation may seem a bit tangled, but the Greek is clear enough):

> ... and causes are spoken of in four senses. In one of these we mean the substance, i.e. the essence (for the 'why' is reducible finally to the definition, and the ultimate 'why' is a cause and principle); in another the matter [30] ... in a third the source of the change ... and in a fourth ... the purpose and the good (for this is the end of all generation and change).[124]

---

123 In an aside suffused with delicacy, our translator of *Physics* exclaimed, "it does violence to the English idiom to call the material out of which a thing is made, or the distinctive attributes which define it, its 'causes,' whereas the Greek *aitia* and the corresponding adjective *aitios* can be applied to anything that is 'guilty of' or 'responsible for' a thing, or 'to the account of which,' for praise or blame, the thing may in any sense be put down. Paraphrase or barbarism offer the only escape from using English words in a sense that they cannot really bear." *The Physics*, trans., Philip A. Wicksteed and Francis M. Cornford. In two volumes. Vol. I: 127. Loeb (Cambridge, MA: Harvard University Press/London: W. Heinemann, 1980).

124 *Metaphysics*, I.3.25-30 (983a).

> ...τὰ δ' αἴτια λέγεται τετραχῶσ, ὧν μίαν μὲν αἰτίαν φαμὲν εἶναι τὴν οὐσιαν καὶ τὸ τί ἦν εἶναι (ἀνάγεται γὰρ τὸ διὰ τί εἰσ τὸν λόγον ἔσχατον, αἴτιον δέ καὶ ἀρχὴ τὸ διὰ τί πρῶτον)...

A bit later, in Book VIII, Aristotle refers to formal cause with these words:

> The formal principle is the definitory formula, but this is obscure if it does not include the cause.[125]
>
> το δ' ὡσ εἶδοσ ὁ λόγοσ, ἀλλὰ ἄδηλοσ ἐὰν μὴ μετὰ τῆσ αἰτίασ ῇ ὁ λόγοσ.

This remark arrives a scant few lines after he had confirmed the identity of formal cause and essence, remarking as follows: τι δ' ως το ειδος; το τι ην ειναι. "What is the formal cause? His essence."[126] By the time of the *Physics,* the pairing of *logos* and *eidos* is so accustomed as to form a hendiadys. In a quick run-through of the causes he gives formal cause as "the 'form' or constituent definition" —ὡσ εἶδοσ καὶ λόγοσ τῶν πραγμάτων".[127] Near the end of *Metaphysics* Aristotle, still using *aitia* for causes in general, reprises the identity of "definition" and *logos,* with "in their universal definition they [causes] are the same": τῷ καθόλου δὲ λόγῳ ταὐτά....[128] St. Thomas Aquinas sums the matter up as follows:

> In another sense cause means the form and pattern of a thing, i.e., its exemplar. This is the

125 *Metaphysics,* VIII.4.10 (1044b).
126 *Metaphysics,* VIII.4.35 (1044a).
127 *Physics,* IV.1.22-23 (209a). Loeb: 282-285.
128 *Metaphysics,* XII.5.29 (1071a).

> formal cause, which is related to a thing in two ways. In one way it stands as the intrinsic form of a thing, and in this respect it is called the formal principle of a thing. In another way it stands as something which is extrinsic to a thing but is that in likeness to which it is made, and in this respect an exemplar is also called a thing's form. It is in this sense that Plato held the Ideas to be forms. Moreover, because it is from its form that each thing derives its nature, whether of its genus or of its species, and the nature of its genus or of its species is what is signified by the definition, which expresses its quiddity, the form of a thing is therefore the intelligible expression of its quiddity, i.e., the formula by which its quiddity is known. For even though certain material parts are given in the definition, still it is from a thing's form that the principal part of the definition comes. The reason why the form is a cause, then, is that it completes the intelligible expression of a thing's quiddity.[129]

The *logos* as constitutive utterance is the same one I wrote about in *Laws of Media*[130] and again in my study of Joyce's *Finnegans Wake, The Role of Thunder.*[131] It is the old, powerful *logos* so eloquently discussed by Eric Havelock,[132] and by Lain-Entralgo in

---

[129] Commentary on the Metaphysics of Aristotle, *Trans., J. P. Rowan (Chicago: Henry Regnery Company, 1961), Book V, Lesson 2, paragraph 764.*

[130] McLuhan and McLuhan, *Op. Cit.*: 35, *ff.*

[131] *The Role of Thunder in* Finnegans Wake (Toronto: University of Toronto Press, 1997).

[132] Havelock, *Plato, Op. Cit.*

Therapy of the Word in Classical Antiquity.[133] The *logos* of a thing was its essential structure or pattern, its mode of being, its definition, its entelechy.[134] Against this, in Aristotle's time, the new alphabet was exercising its influence over the imagination. A new rational mode of *logos* suddenly developed, allowing the older *logos* to come forward to serve as formal cause:

> The term *logos*, richly ambivalent, referring to discourse both as spoken and as written (argument versus treatise) and also to the mental operation (the reasoning power) required to produce it, came into its own, symbolizing the new prosaic and literate discourse (albeit still enjoying a necessary partnership with spoken dialectic). A distinction slowly formed which identified the uttered *epos* of orally-preserved speech as something different from *logos* and (to the philosophers) inferior to it. Concomitantly, the feeling for spoken tongue as a stream flowing (as in Hesiod) was replaced by a vision of a fixed row of letters, and the single word as written, separated from the flow of the

---

[133] Pedro Lain-Entralgo, *Therapy of the Word in Classical Antiquity*, ed. and trans. L. J. Rather and J. M. Sharp (New Haven and London: Yale University Press, 1970).

[134] In *Physics*, II, 3 (195a20-21), Aristotle speaks of *ti en einai*—which he uses there to denote formal cause—as "in the sense of the *essence*—the whole or the synthesis of the form." (*to de holon kai he synthesis kai to eidos.*) Loeb, pp. 132, 133. Also, in *Posterior Analytics*, II, 11 (94a35): "...this is the same as the essence, inasmuch as it is what the definition implies." (*...to ti en einai, to touto semainein ton logon...*) See also *De Anima*: *eti tou dynamei ontos logos he entelecheia* (415a.14-15), "the actuality of that which exists potentially is its essential formula." (*Aristotle: On the Soul, Op. Cit.:* 86, 87 (II.4).

> utterance that contained it, gained recognition as a separate "thing."
>
> There is probably no attestable instance in Greek of the term *logos* as denoting a single "word," though it is often translated as though it did. The first "word for a word" in the early philosophers seems to have been *onoma*—a "name." They recognized that in the orally-preserved speech which they had to use (while striving to correct it) the subjects of significant statements were always persons, with "names," not things or ideas.
>
> As language became separated visually from the person who uttered it, so also the person, the source of the language, came into sharper focus and the concept of selfhood was born. The history of Greek literature is often written as though the concept was already available to Homer and as though it should be taken for granted as a condition of all sophisticated discourse. The early lyric poets of Greece have been interpreted as the voice of an individualism asserting the identities of individual selves, to form a necessary condition of Greek classic culture. This in any strict sense only became true in the time of Plato.[135]

Still in Aristotle's time the mimetic power of the word, as revealed by Havelock in *Preface to Plato* and in *Prologue to Greek Literacy*, was widely experienced and well known enough to be unremarkable, so the notion of verbal transformation and verbal power was equally widely acknowledged. Aristotle says in *De Anima* that

---

135 Eric A. Havelock, *The Muse Learns to Write: Reflections on Orality and Literacy from Antiquity to the Present* (New Haven and London: Yale University Press, 1986): 113.

we all think in images—he takes it for granted, as normal human experience.[136] In the main, comments Ross, Aristotle regards thinking in images "not as a valuable faculty but as a disability, and that is why it never figures, in the *De Anima*, among the main faculties if the soul."[137] If in his time people naturally thought in images, not in words, then an enormous leap in abstract reasoning power would accompany any successful break with image-bound thinking. The syllogism provided the answer: you cannot syllogize with images. It was a method of thinking exclusively with words. Perhaps with great effort you can torture some images into a semblance of a syllogism, but the result is lamentable use of images and nothing like the crisp efficiency of reasoning in words. Aristotle's syllogism constituted a real revolution not only in philosophy but also in making abstract thinking possible.

---

136 "Now for the thinking soul images take the place of direct perceptions; and when it asserts or denies that they are good or bad, it avoids or pursues them. Hence the soul never thinks without a mental image." (Loeb: *Aristotle: On the Soul, Op. Cit.*: 14-17 (III.vii; 481a). The Greek original: *Te de dianoetike psyche ta phantasmata oion aisthemata hyparchei. Otan de agathon he kakon phese he apothese, pheuge he diokei. Dio oudepote noei aneu phantasmatos he psyche...*: τῇ δὲ διανοητικῇ ψυχῇ τὰ φαντάσματα οἷον αἰσθήματα ὑπάρχει, ὅταν δὲ ἀγαθὸν ἢ κακὸν φήσῃ ἢ ἀποφήσῃ, φεύγει ἢ διώκει· διὸ οὐδέποτε νοεῖ ἄνευ φαντάσματος ἡ ψυχή. (Loeb: 176.)

137 *Aristotle, De Anima*, ed., Sir David Ross (Oxford: Clarendon Press, 1961): 39. There is not room here to enter the discussion of modern observations about the "disability" of thinking in images and its relation to split-brain research, although it is absolutely pertinent. At least one extremely suggestive study has discussed thinking in images in relation to autism, which in the present context ought to cast a most illuminating light on Aristotle's difficulties: Lance Strate, *Echoes and Reflections: On Media Ecology as a Field of Study* (Cresskill, NJ: Hampton Press, 2006), especially Part Two.

The syllogism, which made all subsequent philosophy possible, is today obsolete

Dialectic—logic and philosophy—requires that you develop the capacity to think in words, rather than in images. Images are entirely too illogical, too concrete; they do not permit very much in the way of abstraction. As if by magic, Aristotle's syllogism defeats images, freeing the imagination to dance with ideas and words. Could that be a major hidden factor in its significance, to Aristotle & co., and in its essential power? Imagebuster?

When the ancient philosophers averred that the *kosmos* was "informed by" *logos*, they were making a technical statement about a formal cause. The cosmic universe was a verbal universe in which decorum played an essential and excruciatingly delicate part (this situation providing in turn a base for our meanings of "cosmetics"). Decorum is deeply Rhetorical. So the *logos* in question, governed by decorum, is not static but vibrantly active, and therefore it had to have been uttered at some time outside of time (we are in acoustic space now). Utterance presumes an utterer, and in that is matter enough for a separate disquisition: let me just remind the reader of the extensive tradition of commentary on the "Doctrine of the *Logos*." This *logos* is also the same *logos* of creation (*inventio*) as appears in *Genesis* and in the opening of the Last Gospel: 'Εν ἀρχῆ ἦν ὁ λόγοσ, καὶ ὁ λόγοσ ἦν πρὸσ τὸν θεόν, καὶ θεὸσ ἦν ὁ λόγοσ./ *In principio erat Verbum, et Verbum erat apud Deum, et Deus erat Verbum. Hoc erat in principio apud Deum...*

In *Physics*, Book II, Chapter 3, Aristotle uses the now-familiar formula, as he explains that

> the thing in question cannot be there unless the material has actually received the *form* or characteristics of the type, conformity to which brings it within the definition of the thing we say it is, whether specifically or generically.[138]
>
> Ἄλλον δὲ τὸ εἶδοσ καὶ τὸ παράδειγμα. Τοῦτο δ' ἐστὶν ὁ λόγοσ ὁ τοῦ τί ἦν εἶναι καὶ τὰ τούτου γένε

When or how did we become estranged from what Aristotle meant by formal cause? For centuries, philosophy has translated the *logos* of formal cause by the metaphor of "blueprint." After a few moments' reflection you realize that the "blueprint" image puts all the stress on arrangement, *dispositio*. Thereby, translators & philosophers have flang one humungous and odoriferous red herring across the path, wedged it up the innocent's nose... "Blueprint" is powerfully visual: such a picture-drawing of the sizes and positions of components *vis-à-vis* each other is *dispositio* in full regalia. On the surface, "blueprint," and the translation "rational plan" for *logos*, do have a little in common.[139] Marcus Long spells out the "house" illustration of the four causes:

---

138 *Physics, Op. Cit.*: 129; the Greek version is on p. 128.

139 Translators continually struggle to render *logos*, for which English has no adequate equivalent. Also lacking one, Latin resorted to the hendiadys, *ratio atque oratio*, which they understood as "wisdom and eloquence" and used as a foundation for the alliance of Grammar and Rhetoric. The translator of *Generation of Animals* remarks in a note, that "we have here a term of wide and varied application, with which a number of

> ...there is a material cause for everything, in the Aristotelian sense that there is something which is potentially something else. In order to build a house we must have bricks or stones or wood. These are the house not actually but potentially, and therefore represent the *material* cause.
>
> Bricks or wood or stones have no capacity to shape themselves into houses; for this we need a carpenter or a bricklayer or a stonemason. It is through the efforts of such men that the material cause can assume a certain form. Such men, then, are the *efficient* cause or that which produces the effect, in this case a house.
>
> A bricklayer, to confine our illustration to him, does not pick up the bricks and throw them together at random, hoping for the best. He always has a plan or blueprint to guide him in the construction. This blueprint represents the form that is to be realized it is the organizing principle. In the Aristotelian doctrine it is the form that actualizes the potentiality, making the thing the sort of thing it is. This is the *formal* cause.

---

correlated conceptions are associated, one or other of which may be uppermost in a particular case. The fundamental idea of [*logos*], as its connexion with [*legein*] shows, is that of *something spoken or uttered,* more especially a *rational utterance* or *rational explanation,* expressing a thing's *nature* and the *plan* of it; hence [*logos*] can denote the *defining formula,* the *definition* of a thing's *essence,* of its *essential being* (as often in the phrase [*logos tes ousias*]), expressing the structure or character of the object to be defined." Aristotle: *Generation of Animals,* trans. A. L. Peck (Cambridge, MA: Harvard University Press/London: William Heinemann Ltd., 1963): xliv. This is the new (conventional) translation, not the manifold, transformative *logos* of the pre-Socratics.

We do not collect material and hire a bricklayer to build a certain type of house without some purpose in mind. We may want the house for our own dwelling, or to rent as an investment, or simply to be a garage or storehouse. It is clear that these purposes will play a large part in determining the type of material used and the sort of workmen hired. Nothing is done without a purpose. The word "purpose" comes from a Greek word *telos* meaning literally the *end* or *goal*. Insofar as we stress the purposive causes we are said to be speaking teleologically. In the pattern of the analysis of causality in Aristotle this is called the *final* cause.

There are, then, according to Aristotle, four causes involved in the explanation of the development of any object, the material, the efficient, the formal and the final. These four causes are related to Aristotle's discussion of matter and form. The material cause as potentiality is the same as matter, whereas the other causes are an expansion of the meaning of form or actuality. Of these three causes, the final cause was the most important for Aristotle, who thought of the purpose, or goal, of development as the real reason for the thing.

The expression "final cause" suggests that the present is determined by the future, in the sense that it is what a thing is to become that determines the present stage of its development. We should be misunderstanding the meaning of the term and raising unnecessary difficulties if we supposed that a nonexistent future is the cause of the existent present. There must be a meaning of final cause other than a merely temporal one. That

> meaning is found in the general nature of the form of the thing if considered in its timeless aspect.[140]

Aristotle, in *Metaphysics*, puts the entire matter somewhat more succinctly:

> The same thing may have all the kinds of causes, e.g. the moving cause of a house is the art or the builder, the final cause is the function it fulfils, the matter is earth and stones, and the form is the definition.[141]
>
> ἐνδέχεται γὰρ τῷι αὐτῷι πάντασ τοὺσ τρόπουσ τοὺσ τῶν αἰτίων ὑπάρχειν, οἷον οἰκίασ ὅθεν μὲν ἡ κινησισ ἡ τέχνη καὶ ὁ οἰκοδόμοσ, οὗ δ' ἕνεκα τὸ ἔργον, ὕλη δὲ γῆ καὶ λίθοι, τὸ δ' εἶδοσ ὁ λόγοσ.

Again the familiar pairing of form (*eidos*) and *logos*. This *logos* is clearly light-years removed from the passivity conveyed by our conventional translation: "blueprint." Marcus Long does point out, though, that "in the Aristotelian doctrine it is the form that actualizes the potentiality, making the thing the sort of thing it is." At bottom, formal cause is coercive, not passive. It *makes* the thing. It, as it were, shoves it into *being*, and it makes it be *thus*.

Etienne Gilson brought this matter clearly to view when commenting on St. Thomas's "reform of metaphysics": Thomas introduced

> a clear-cut distinction between the two orders of formal causality and efficient causality.

[140] Marcus Long, *The Spirit of Philosophy* (Toronto: University of Toronto Press, 1953): 142-143.
[141] Book III, Chapter 2, 996b.5.

> Formal causality is that which makes things to be *what* they are, and, in a way, it also makes them to be, since, in order to be, each and every being has to be a *what.* But formal causality dominates the whole realm of substance, and its proper effect is substantiality, whereas efficient causality is something quite different... It is, then, literally true to say that existence is a consequence which follows from the form of essence, but not as an effect follows from the efficient cause...[142] In short, forms are "formal" causes of existence, to the whole extent to which they contribute to the establishment of substances which are capable of existing.[143]

Gilson emphasizes: "No point could be more clearly stated than is this one in the metaphysics of Thomas Aquinas. The form truly is 'cause of being' for that subject in which it is, and it is not such owing to another form (*forma non habet sic esse per aliam formam*)."[144] Thomas cleared up the reciprocal relation between formal and efficient causalities,[145] reflected in the ancient saw, "*causae ad invicem causae sunt, sed in diverso genere.*" Causes cause causes. But the blurring remained in some minds and continued to cause trouble.

The "blueprint" metaphor gave Dialecticians—Philosophers—what they needed to make formal cause behave rationally. That powerful image immediately invests the imaginations of those who have been exposed to it, and it has related formal cause indelibly

---

[142] *Thomas Aquinas,* Qu. Disp. De Anima*, art. 14, ad 4m. Cf. Ad 5 m; and* In Boethium de Trinitate*, q. V, art. 4, ad 4m, ed. P. Wyser, p. 50, l. 19-p. 51, l. 11. (Gilson's note.)*

[143] Gilson, *Being and Some Philosophers, Op. Cit.*: 168-169.

[144] *Op. Cit.*: 170.

[145] See Gilson's discussion, *Op. Cit.*: 172, ff.

to *dispositio.* Disposition—arrangement—is perilously close to sequence and efficient cause. That blasted "blueprint" carries with it a specifically and emphatically visual bias. A blueprint details for the eye how matters are or ought to be disposed. And still, formal cause resists the pressure to turn rational and continues to live in the world of *inventio* and *elocutio* and decorum—all of them fluid and irrational.

Exasperated by the "rational" formal cause which philosophy handed down, Heidegger had to reinvent and rename it

Martin Heidegger confronted this contaminated sense of formal cause when he raised *The Question Concerning Technology,*[146] and rejected it as inadequate to his needs. In its place he posited "Enframing," as the essence of the manner in which new technologies operate on cultures. It is clear from what he says that with "Enframing" he is trying his best to convey what Aristotle meant by formal cause

[146] *The Question Concerning Technology and Other Essays, Translated and with an Introduction by William Levitt* (New York: Harper Colophon Books, 1977). Heidegger provides an extended criticism of the four causes as received, which he regards nevertheless as indispensable to understanding technological transformations of culture.

and *logos* (definition, essence, entelechy). He has simply found the term formal cause so polluted by usage in his time as to be nearly useless. Consider, for example, the passage,

> The essence of technology lies in *Logos*. Its holding-sway belongs within destining. Since destining at any given time starts man on a way of revealing, man, thus under way, is continually approaching the brink of the possibility of pursuing and pushing forward nothing but what is revealed in ordering, and of deriving all his standards on this basis. Through this, the other possibility is blocked, that man might be admitted more and sooner and ever more primally to the essence of that which is unconcealed and to its unconcealment, in order that he might experience as his essence his needed belonging to revealing.
>
> ...Man stands so decisively in attendance on the challenging-forth of *Logos* that he does not apprehend *Logos* as a claim, that he fails to see himself as the one spoken to, and hence also fails in every way to hear in what respect he ek-sists, from out of his essence, in the realm of exhortation or address, and thus *can never* encounter only himself.
>
> But *Logos* does not simply endanger man in his relationship to himself and to everything that is. As a destining, it banishes man into that kind of revealing which is an ordering. Where this ordering holds sway, it drives out every other possibility of revealing. Above all, *Logos* conceals that revealing which, in the sense of *poiēsis*, lets what presences come forth into appearance. ... Where *Logos*

> holds sway, regulating and securing of the standing-reserve mark all revealing. They no longer even let their own fundamental characteristic appear, namely, this revealing as such.
>
> Thus the challenging *Logos* not only conceals a former way of revealing, bringing-forth, but it conceals revealing itself and with it That wherein unconcealment, i.e., truth, comes to pass.[147]

Had Aristotle written in modern German and been subjected to the tortures of philosophical translation, the result might very well have resembled this text. I have made just one alteration to it: I have substituted "Logos" where Heidegger has put "Enframing." By "standing reserve" he evidently means a residue of possible forms. His struggle to invent formal cause, however, illuminates one of the problems to which phenomenology as a whole is a response. For centuries since the scholastics, Dialectic has relied on the other causes and found them adequate to solving questions of figures minus grounds. But electric circuitry banishes uniformity and now we have several ground transformations per decade. This alone is enough to present philosophy with an urgent need for formal cause as a way to approach the world of electric technology.

The formal cause of a painting or a poem or an advertisement is the audience for which it was made and on which it is to operate. Northrop Frye is exactly wrong: the formal cause MUST exist outside the painting or the poem, prior to it. Here is Frye's statement in *Anatomy of Criticism*:

---

[147] Heidegger, *Op. Cit.*: 26-27.

> An original painter knows, of course, that when the public demands likeness to an object, it generally wants the exact opposite, likeness to the pictorial conventions it is familiar with. Hence when he breaks with these conventions, he is often apt to assert that he is nothing but an eye, that he merely paints what he sees as he sees it, and the like. His motive in talking such nonsense is clear enough: he wishes to say that painting is not merely facile decoration, and involves a difficult conquest of some very real spatial problems. But this may be freely admitted without agreeing that the formal cause of a picture is outside the picture, an assertion which would destroy the whole art if it were taken seriously.[148]

Frye is in trouble, and knows it: the formal cause of the poem is the reader; of the speech or the ad, the audience—and all exist "outside" the thing. Frye's remarks, somewhat later, in *Fables of Identity* help understand where he went off the rails:

> There is still before us the problem of the formal cause of the poem, a problem deeply involved with the question of genres. We cannot say much about genres, for criticism does not know much about them. A good many critical efforts to grapple with such words as "novel" or "epic" are chiefly interesting as examples of the

---

[148] *Anatomy of Criticism—Four Essays* (Princeton, NJ: Princeton University Press, 1957): 132. Compare Gilson, *Op. Cit.*, p. 174: "In short, form is the cause of actual existence, inasmuch as it is the formal cause of the substance which receives its own act of existing. This is why, as Thomas Aquinas so often says, *esse consequitur formam*: to be follows upon form." And p. 175: "In order to receive its to be, a form must needs be in potency to it. 'To be,' then, is the act of the form, not *qua* form, but *qua* being."

> psychology of rumor. Two conceptions of the genre, however, are obviously fallacious, and as they are opposite extremes, the truth must lie somewhere between them. One is the pseudo-Platonic conception of genres as existing prior to and independently of creation, which confuses them with mere conventions of form like the sonnet. The other is that pseudo-biological conception of them as evolving species which turns up in so many surveys of the "development" of this or that form.[149]

McLuhan responded to Frye with *From Cliché to Archetype*, a study of the dynamics of formal causes and their relation to the retrieval process. The dust jacket announces the main theme:

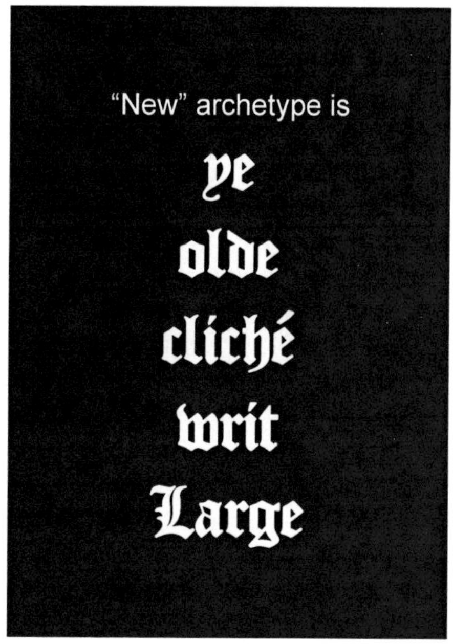

"New" archetype is
ye
olde
cliché
writ
Large

[149] *Fables of Identity: Studies in Poetic Mythology* (New York: Harcourt, Brace & World, Inc.): 11.

At his back, Frye has a centuries-long misunderstanding of formal cause.

The search for forms—formal causes—united grammarians' labors in both the written text and the book of nature

Francis Bacon adamantly insisted that all study of final causes be dropped, as it was corrupting the science of his time. He turned his own attention from armchair theorizing to rooting out formal causes, based on observation and collecting empirical evidence.[150] Nature, as much as literature, constitutes an encyclopaedia, so the grammarian of any age needed to bring to bear the full trivium and quadrivium as well as keen perception and critical faculties. They use the arts and sciences to penetrate the Book of Nature and recover knowledge, lost at the Fall, of the languages in which it is written. Each act of reading in either Book was therefore an act of meditation that required simultaneous awareness of all levels and causes and their interrelations.[151]

[150] For a delightful history of final causation (teleological cause), see Etienne Gilson's *From Aristotle to Darwin and Back Again: A Journey in Final Causality, Species, and Evolution* (Notre Dame, Indiana: University of Notre Dame Press, 1984).

[151] See Ivan Illich, *In the Vineyard of the Text: A Commentary to Hugh of St. Victor's* Didascalion (Chicago and London: University of

Grammar brings all of her tools of etymology and formal analysis to bear on decoding and reading the Two Books.

> Bacon opens Book II of his *Novum Organum* with a report on the state of understanding in each of the four departments of causality.[152]
>
>> The unhappy state of man's actual knowledge is manifest . . . It is rightly laid down that true knowledge is that which is deduced from causes. The division of four causes also is not amiss: matter, form, the efficient, and end or final cause. Of these, however, the latter is so far from being beneficial, that it even corrupts the sciences . . . The discovery of form is considered

---

Chicago Press, 1993): 51 ff. Reading was far from passive, and recommended throughout antiquity as strenuous exercise: "Hellenistic physicians prescribed reading as an alternative to ball playing or a walk. Reading presupposed that you be in good physical form; the frail or infirm were not supposed to read with their own tongue. At one solstice, Nicholas of Clairvaux had submitted with all the other monks to the customary quarterly purging and bleeding, but this time the fast in combination with the cupping had left him too weak for a while to continue his reading. When Peter the Venerable had a cold which made him cough when he opened his mouth, he could not read, neither in the choir nor in his cell 'to himself.'" (57-58). He notes: "The most readable and dense description of monastic reading is still Jean Leclerq, *Love of Learning,* especially '*Lectio and Meditatio,*' pp. 15-17, where these two anecdotes and their sources are given." (58.) See Jean Leclerq, *The Love of Learning and the Desire for God* (New York: Fordham University Press, 1982).

[152] This passage is taken from my essay, "Francis Bacon's Theory of Communication," *Going for Baroque: Cultural Transformations 1550-1650,* ed. Francesco Guardiani (Brooklyn, NY: Legas, 1999): 26-27.

> desperate. As for the efficient cause and matter . . . they are but desultory and superficial, and of scarcely any avail to real and active knowledge.

The discovery of form united all labours on the Two Books; for, as held throughout the tradition, the forms manifest the Logos and provide the common language in which both Books are inscribed. They serve not as the *figure* but the *ground* of matter, and they underlie the analogical ratios between the Two Books. In this regard, etymology provides a major technique of scientific investigation. The whole aim of the arts and sciences therefore is to enable the discovery and understanding, and ultimately the manipulation (alchemy) of forms. This constitutes media study of a high order. The great alchemists, the Paracelsans from Raymond Lully to Cornelius Agrippa, were grammarians. Bacon is perfectly aware of how the sciences and arts are united by the study of forms and formal causes:

> On a given basis of matter to impose any nature, within the limits of possibility, is the intention of human power. In like manner, to know the causes of a given effect, in whatever subject, is the intention of human knowledge: which intentions coincide. For that which is in contemplation as a cause, is in operation as a medium....
>
> He who knows the efficient and materiate causes, composes or divides things previously invented, or transfers and produces them; also in matter

> somewhat similar, he attaineth unto new inventions; the more deeply fixed limits of things he moveth not.
>
> He who knows the forms, discloses and educes things which have not hitherto been done, such as neither the vicissitudes of nature, nor the diligence of experience might ever have brought into action, or as might not have entered into man's thoughts.[153]

Laws of Media: The New Science also concerns this area of formal causality. Our tetrad of laws[154] brings Aristotle up to date; at the same time, it provides an analytic of formal cause, the first ever proposed. Because the tetrads apply exclusively to human utterances and artifacts, it follows that formal cause is uniquely and particularly human. That is, and I believe this to be crucial, absent human agency or intellect there is no formal cause at all.[155] Certainly

---

153 Tract entitled "Francis Bacon's Aphorisms and Advices Concerning the Helps of the Mind and the Kindling of Natural Light." *The Works of Francis Bacon, Lord Chancellor of England. A New edition: with a Life of the Author, by Basil Montagu, Esq.*, In Three Volumes (Philadelphia: Parry & McMillan, 1854): Vol. I, 454.

154 You can apply the four laws (we state them as questions) to any human artefact, hardware or software alike. What does the thing set aside / obsolesce? What much older thing does it retrieve / update in a new form? What, already present, does it amplify / enhance? What complementary form does it reverse into / put on when pushed too far? These four laws have among themselves the ratios of proper proportionality—a is to b as c is to d—that characterize the *logos*, and every word, and the nature of metaphor. There is no sequence: they apply simultaneously. They bridge the hitherto separate worlds of technology and the arts.

155 This explains the difficulties facing anyone who tries to discern formal causes in Nature or to separate them there from final causes. Cf. the remarks in the Great Books' explanation (used above):

all of the elements of the tetrad, the four processes, are both formal and causal. And *con*formal. And I have elsewhere discussed the tetrad's identity with *logos* and definition.[156] The deep structure or "definition" of a thing is to be found in the nature and interaction of the four simultaneous processes, amplification, obsolescence, retrieval, and reversal. Together they enact the verbal role of metaphor—*logos*. Some of that is in *Laws of Media*. Together, the four processes of the tetrad spell out the entelechy—and aetiology—of their subject. They give its Grammar and nature. The active part of the *logos*, the transforming part, is the province of Rhetoric. Entelechies, just as clearly, side with etymology and manifold simultaneous levels of existence—and analogy as regards being, whether considered modally or absolutely. The word *entelechy*, Aristotle's coinage, serves as the central conception of the *De Anima*.[157] (Always bearing in mind the crucial distinctions between Divine and human agency, and between uttering and re-uttering, and between cognition and recognition: "mirabilius condidisti et mirabiliter reformasti." Adam's first job in the Garden was the naming of creatures.)

> But the formal cause is not as apparent in nature as in art. Whereas in art it can be identified by reference to the plan in the maker's mind, it must be discovered in nature in the change itself, as that which completes the process. For example the redness which the apple takes on in ripening is the formal cause of its alteration in color. The trouble with the final cause is that it so often tends to be inseparable from the formal cause; for unless some extrinsic purpose can be found for a natural change—some end beyond itself which the change serves—the final cause, or that for the sake of which the change took place, is no other than the quality or form which the matter assumes as a result of its transformation.

[156] See McLuhan and McLuhan, *Op. Cit.*

[157] See *Aristotle, De Anima*, Ed., Sir David Ross (Oxford: Clarendon Press, 1961): 10. On p. 11 he supplies a complete list of the occurrences of the word *entelecheia* in Aristotle's works.

Single-level existence, stripped of all discontinuities, in these precincts, means death; and exactly that rarefied and sanitized locus of operation is the heaven of Dialectic: visual space. All modes and kinds of being, including our own, as we know, derive by analogy from the supreme Being; analogy requires discontinuity, not connectedness or logic. In that sense, we are all made "in the image and likeness..." meaning, by analogy. However, here let me address the imputation that McLuhan was involved in some form of determinism. His aim was always to explore and document and interpret the operation of formal causes, the making process at work in literature and in culture. He had no particular interest in efficient cause or final cause—either of which is in its own manner the domain of "determinism," and both of which are concerns of normal science.

What, then, is the main reason Dialectic has such difficulty with formal cause? It could be because formal cause is irrational, and Dialectic is above all else rational. Formal cause has other properties that Dialectic would find unwelcome: it is not sequential (it operates outside of chronological time, which in and of itself offends rationality), and it is too low definition, because it can never be hotted up to play *figure* to some other *ground*. Having no points of contact with Dialectic, therefore, it does not "belong to" Dialectic, neither does it belong in or with or around Dialectic. Formal cause is an *auslander*; it emanates from Grammar and Rhetoric at their most elemental and most profound. Moreover, etymology lies at the root of the grammatical instinct. Grammar has its roots in *the logos spermatikos*, the seeds of things and words and their formal structures. (Hence Grammar's two main areas of activity: etymology and interpretation of texts.) Dialectic, on the other hand, grows out of the *logos hendiathetos*, the unspoken "word" in the mind, the thought process abstracted from utterance and from hearer. The silent word.[158] Rhetoric itself derives from the *logos prophorikos*, the uttered word that goes forth to transform the hearer. A Dialectician seeks to change your mind, to convince you; a Rhetorician, rather, aims to change *you*, to modify *how* you think rather than *what* you think. Blended together, these three modes of *logos* together constitute the old *logos* of the pre-Socratics and considerably pre-Aristotle and pre-Plato. Reborn separately as the trivium they have shaped our Western intellectual tradition from Roman times to the present.

Formal cause is in the end of no interest to Dialecticians because they have no use for it. It does not apply to things of the mind, it solves no problems for them; it poses no answers—or questions—that they are disposed to entertain. Formal cause concerns the *ground* as seedbed, as active process. Or if not exactly the *ground* then (much the same thing) the interval between *figure* and *ground*, so that the formal cause is also the conformal cause, as it were, and is the cause of the *figure* and its *ground* simultaneously.[159] That interval full of active interface is an active process of formation and counterformation, yet it is not diachronic. The restless pressures and counterpressures perform their isometric dance—with no need of uniform tempo, no

---

158 Plato's Ideas, his ideal forms are mental images. They would appear natural consorting with the word in the mind before speech; some images may not be spoken as verbal embodiments are still inadequate. By contrast, Aristotle's *logos* as formal cause clearly associates with an embodied word. Gilson warns (*Being and Some Philosophers, Op. Cit.*: 183): "To posit essence or supreme essentiality as the supreme degree of reality is therefore the most disastrous of all metaphysical mistakes, because it is to substitute *essentia* for *esse* as the ultimate root of all being. The whole of metaphysics is here at stake..."

159 See below, T. S. Eliot on "Tradition and the Individual Talent."

need of uniform time. Ironically, although three-quarters of Aristotle's tetrad of causes operate outside time, formal cause alone is reckoned irrational. The modality of formal cause is that of abrasive interface, an exchange of pressures and textures between situations: consequently, it belongs to touch, kinesis, and proprioception. This is a world of constant isometric compression and tension. Material cause too is extratemporal; that is, time may be present but its chronological aspect is incidental at best, or simply irrelevant. Matter always needs being, but clearly does not always need becoming.[160] Final cause, too, is extratemporal. One has to make a constant effort to bear in mind that the final cause (that for the sake of which, as 'Arry continually reminds us; also, the end—*telos*—or purpose) is NOT the end-point of a chain or series of efficient causes. Final cause is present *in toto* from the outset, even before the sequence of making gets underway. The world of final cause, then, functions outside of chronological time. Yet it too is not considered irrational—which indicates that it too is presently misunderstood.

There is this important difference between efficient cause and final cause as regards time and temporality. Final cause does not lie at the end of a series of efficient causes because it is present in its entirety from the outset. It is, after all, not a result but a cause. It lies outside chronological time: it does not admit of degrees of completion. If chronology belongs to efficient cause, infinity belongs to final cause because infinity too is not gradual but sudden. There are no degrees of infinitude. Infinity too functions to one side of chronological time, an absolute. Final

[160] Or unbecoming, but not decay. Decay belongs to transformation; unbecoming—one-half the process of decay—does not.

cause is absolute and simultaneous; it anticipates the chronological making process. Like infinity, it anticipates time. Formal cause, on the other hand, is not infinite but de-finite. Bound up in definition, it has no need for chronological time. And like final cause, formal cause concerns being. Formal cause, because it is absolute, does not admit of degrees.

Bad art results whenever the artist con-fuses formal cause and one of the other causes (usually final cause)

Although he refrains from mentioning it by name, T. S. Eliot was much concerned with formal cause in his musings on poetry and poetics. It was integral to his theory of communication. In a meditation on "The Frontiers of Criticism," he offers this contrast between the material (subject matter used as material cause), efficient cause (producer and production), and formal cause, as regards poetry:

> ...One can explain a poem by investigating what it is made of and the causes that brought it about; and explanation may be a necessary preparation for understanding. But to understand a poem it is also necessary, and I should say in most instances still more necessary, that we should endeavour to grasp what the poetry is aiming to be; one might

> say—though it is long since I have employed such terms with any assurance—endeavouring to grasp its entelechy.[161]

Aristotle uses "entelechies" to denote primal causes.[162] Human understanding is inseparable from the formal cause of the poem as an active force. Some reader or critic must provide the understanding. Poems are not isolated objects, like consumer goods, but active processes that complete—achieve—their forms by interacting with audiences. **The reader is the formal cause of the poem.** And the audience is the formal cause of the advertisement, sculpture, song, or sofa—and the consumer of the consumer product. Joyce: "My consumers are they not my producers?"[163] A parallel term for entelechy might be vortex, as used above. Marshall McLuhan's idea of a medium as an invisible, ever-present vortex of services and disservices is exactly that of formal cause. As he wrote,

> [Frederick Wilhelmsen] is interested in working on St. Thomas' theory of communication, and I have pointed out to him that Aquinas designates his audience, the people he wants to influence and alter, in the Objections of each article. Then I realized that the audience is, in all matters of art and expression, the formal cause, e.g., fallen man is the formal cause of

---

161 *On Poetry and Poets* (New York: Noonday Press/Farrar, Straus & Cudahy, 1943): 122.

162 *Cf.*, "eti to prôton entelecheiai" (*Metaphysics*, XII.5.35—1071a).

163 *Finnegans Wake*, 497.01. Joyce is a prime source of insight into the workings of formal cause, in literature as in life. *Finnegans Wake* is a formal teaching machine. To approach it in search of meanings in the ordinary sense is to miss the point entirely.

> the Incarnation, and Plato's public is the formal cause of his philosophy. Formal cause is concerned with effects and with structural form, and not with value judgments.
>
> My own approach to the media has been entirely from formal cause. Since formal causes are hidden and environmental, they exert their structural pressure by interval and interface with whatever is in their environmental territory. Formal cause[s are] always hidden, whereas the things upon which they act are visible. The TV generation has been shaped not by TV programs, but by the pervasive and penetrating character of the TV image, or service, itself.[164]

A bad poem results from con-fusing—fusing together or merging—its formal and final causes. What Eliot said of the bad poet is true also of the reader of a bad poem: Eliot maintained that the inferior poet is conscious where he ought to be unconscious, and unconscious where he ought to be conscious: the same mix-up happens to the reader of a bad poem. The inferior poem draws your attention to itself and its language, its tricks and devices, then does nothing,

---

[164] Letter, written 19 June, 1975, to Fr. John Culkin. *Letters, Op. Cit.*: 510. Wihelmsen had written, in *The Paradoxical Structure of Existence*: "Both Plato and Aristotle attempted to seek the roots of form and both men found them in different "locations" so to speak. Plato saw the relation between forms and things as initiating in the mind and as terminating in things. Form enjoys, in Platonism, a primacy and a priority in mind. Initially, forms are 'in themselves,' intellected within the human spirit; afterwards, and only afterwards, forms are understood as being in things which participate in them in partial and imperfect ways. Plato insisted, hence, that an order of the forms of being is implied in the very act of thinking: forms of being are the meanings of being" *Op. Cit.*: 17. In short, in Plato, the medium is the message.

leaving you numb in that quarter. Or it tries to convince you of some doctrine. Either way, it attempts to force-fit the formal cause inside the poem.

The poem by itself, in the abstract, is comparatively meaningless. Saying that the poem cannot be fully understood until you have taken into account the poet and the circumstances of the poem's creation is like saying that you can't understand the car—or a given car—until you have taken into account Detroit and the influences on, and actions of, and intentions of, all of the people who toiled to produce the car—the makers. Here we see that little tyrant, efficient cause, asserting itself.

> For myself, I can only say that a knowledge of the springs which released a poem is not necessarily a help towards understanding the poem: too much information about the origins of a poem may even break my contact with it. I feel no need for any light upon the Lucy poems beyond the radiance shed by the poems themselves.
>
> ...It is relevant if we want to understand Wordsworth; but it is not directly relevant to our understanding of his poetry. Or rather it is not relevant to our understanding of *the poetry as poetry*. I am even prepared to suggest that there is, in all great poetry, something which must remain unaccountable however complete might be our knowledge of the poet, and that that is what matters most. When the poem has been made, something new has happened, something that cannot be wholly explained by

> anything that went before. That, I believe, is what we mean by 'creation.'[165]

Wallace Stevens went Eliot one better when he performed his field experiment of formal cause. Here is the lab report he wrote, in the form of the poem, "The Anecdote of the Jar":

> I placed a jar in Tennessee
> And round it was, upon a hill.
> It made the slovenly wilderness
> Surround that hill.
>
> The wilderness rose up to it
> And sprawled around, no longer wild.
> The jar was round upon the ground
> And tall and of a port in air.
>
> It took dominion everywhere.
> The jar was gray and bare.
> It did not give of bird or bush,
> Like nothing else in Tennessee.

The jar provided the formal cause of all of the metamorphoses mentioned in the poem. (Considered in terms merely of the matter or actions of the agent, the poem simply concerns an act of littering.) This poem is the only example I know of where a poet, or artist of any ilk, consciously performed a perceptual experiment and reported the results in verse.

Early in his career, Eliot published a personal manifesto of sorts under the title of "Tradition and the Individual Talent." It is his own case-study of formal cause in the area of poetics. First, he establishes the acoustic nature of the Tradition as a set of

---

[165] Eliot, *On Poetry, Op. Cit.*: 124.

simultaneous relations, *not* a sequence or parade of big reputations:

> Tradition is a matter of much wider significance. It cannot be inherited, and if you want it you must obtain it by great labour. It involves, in the first place, the historical sense, which we may call nearly indispensable to anyone who would continue to be a poet beyond his twenty-fifth year; and the historical sense involves a perception, not only of the pastness of the past, but of its presence; the historical sense compels a man to write not merely with his own generation in his bones, but with a feeling that the whole of the literature of Europe from Homer and within it the whole of the literature of his own country has a simultaneous existence and composes a simultaneous order. The historical sense, which is a sense of the timeless as well as of the temporal and of the timeless and of the temporal together, is what makes a writer traditional. And it is at the same time what makes a writer most acutely conscious of his place in time, of his contemporaneity.[166]

The historical sense provides the appropriate perceptual stance, the requisite sensitivity. In the next sentences, Eliot puts formal cause on display as he details the process of conforming or mutual forming of the individual talent and the tradition:

---

[166] "Tradition and the Individual Talent," from *The Sacred Wood: Essays on Poetry and Criticism* (London: Methuen, 1920): 47-59. These remarks, 49.

> No poet, no artist of any art, has his complete meaning alone. His significance, his appreciation is the appreciation of his relation to the dead poets and artists. You cannot value him alone; you must set him, for contrast and comparison, among the dead. I mean this as a principle of aesthetic, not merely historical, criticism. The necessity that he shall conform, that he shall cohere, is not one-sided; what happens when a new work of art is created is something that happens simultaneously to all the works of art which preceded it. The existing monuments form an ideal order among themselves, which is modified by the introduction of the new (the really new) work of art among them. The existing order is complete before the new work arrives; for order to persist after the supervention of novelty, the *whole* existing order must be, if ever so slightly, altered; and so the relations, proportions, values of each work of art toward the whole are readjusted; and this conformity between the old and the new. Whoever has approved this idea of order, of the form of European, or English literature, will not find it preposterous that the past should be altered by the present as much as the present is dictated by the past. And the poet who is aware of this will be aware of great difficulties and responsibilities.[167]

In a word: the individual talent is the formal cause of the tradition. This finding is of the same order as that "*logos* is the formal cause of the *cosmos*" (see Appendix One, *infra*).

---

[167] *Ibid.*: 49-50.

Ezra Pound found formal cause everywhere at work when he wrote about "The Serious Artist." The métier of the arts is the culture's sense and sensibility; the artist's particular job, which only he is trained for, is to report on it as exactly as possible.

> This brings us to the immorality of bad art. Bad art is inaccurate art. It is art that makes false reports. If a scientist falsifies a report either deliberately or through negligence we consider him as either a criminal or a bad scientist according to the enormity of his offence, and he is punished or despised accordingly.
>
> If he falsifies the reports of a maternity hospital in order to retain his position and get profit and advancement from the city board, he may escape detection. If he declines to make such falsification he may lose financial rewards, and in either case his baseness or his pluck may pass unknown and unnoticed save by a very few people. Nevertheless one does not have to argue his case. The layman knows soon enough on hearing it whether the physician is to be blamed or praised.
>
> If the artist falsifies his report as to the nature of man, as to his own nature, as to the nature of his ideal of the perfect, as to the nature of his ideal of this, that or the other, of god, if god exist, of the force with which he believes or disbelieves this, that or the other, of the degree in which he suffers or is made glad; if the artist falsifies his reports on these matters or on any other matter in order that he may conform to the taste of his time, to the proprieties of a sovereign, to the conveniences of a preconceived code of ethics, then that artist

lies. If he lies out of deliberate will to lie, if he lies out of carelessness, out of laziness, out of cowardice, out of any sort of negligence whatsoever, he nevertheless lies and he should be punished or despised in proportion to the seriousness of his offence. His offence is of the same nature as the physician's and according to his position and the nature of his lie he is responsible for future oppressions and future misconceptions. Albeit his lies are known to only a few, or his truth-telling to only a few. Albeit he may pass without censure for the one and without praise for the other...

We distinguish very clearly between the physician who is doing his best for a patient, who is using drugs in which he believes, or who is in a wilderness, let us say, where the patient can get no other medical aid. We distinguish, I say, very clearly between the failure of such a physician, and the act of that physician, who ignorant of the patient's disease, being in reach of more skilful physicians, deliberately denies an ignorance of which he is quite conscious, refuses to consult other physicians, tries to prevent the patient's having access to more skilful physicians, or deliberately tortures the patient for his own ends.

One does not need to read black print to learn this ethical fact about physicians. Yet it takes a deal of talking to convince a layman that bad art is "immoral". And that good art however "immoral" it is, is wholly a thing of virtue. Purely and simply that good art can NOT be immoral. By good art I mean art that bears

> true witness, I mean the art that is most precise.[168]

So the arts draw their form from the perceptions and sensibilities of the culture, and this process also plays in the artist's "putting on" his audience. The *ground* always provides the formal cause of its *figures*.

In his poem "Esthétique du Mal" Wallace Stevens sings of the embrace of forms:

> This is the thesis scrivened in delight,
> The reverberating psalm, the right chorale.
>
> One might have thought of sight, but who could
> think
> Of what it sees, for all the ill it sees?
> Speech found the ear, for all the evil sound,
> But the dark italics it could not propound.
> And out of what one sees and hears and out
> Of what one feels, who could have thought to
> make
> So many selves, so many sensuous worlds,
> As if the air, the mid-day air, was swarming
> With the metaphysical changes that occur,
> Merely in living as and where we live.

He indicates that the slightest shift in the level of visual intensity produces a subtle modulation in our sense of our selves, both private and corporate. Since technologies extend our own physiology, they result in new programs of an environmental kind. Such pervasive experiences as those deriving from the encounter with environments almost inevitably escape

---

[168] "The Serious Artist," in *Literary Essays of Ezra Pound, edited by T. S. Eliot* (New York: New Directions, 1968): 43-44.

perception. The formal causes of perception—and imperception[169]—they are made visible only by the action of a counter-environment.

> When two or more environments encounter one another by direct interface, they tend to manifest their distinctive qualities. Comparison and contrast have always been a means of sharpening perception in the arts as well as in general experience. Indeed, it is upon this pattern that all the structures of art have been reared. Any artistic endeavor includes the preparing of an environment for human attention. A poem or a painting is in every sense a teaching machine for the training of perception and judgment. The artist is a person who is especially aware of the challenge and dangers of new environments presented to human sensibility. Whereas the ordinary person seeks security by numbing his perception against the impact of new experience, the artist delights in this novelty and instinctively creates situations that both reveal it and compensate for it. The artist studies the distortion of sensory life produced by new environmental programming and tends to create artistic situations that correct the sensory bias and derangement brought about by the new form. In social terms the artist can be regarded as a navigator who gives adequate compass bearings in spite of magnetic deflection of the needle by the changing play of

---

[169] Francis Bacon has articulated the formal causes of imperception in his doctrine of the four Idols, taken from his medieval kinsman, Roger Bacon. Whereas the four causes do cause something, the Idols are forms of inertia, death, uncausing, noncausing.

> forces. So understood, the artist is not a peddler of new ideals or lofty experiences. He is rather the indispensable aid to action and reflection alike.[170]

If the vortex of effects arrives first then we can escape it, as Poe suggests, only by formal, structural study of its action. We can manipulate any environmental vortex by judicial design of counter-environments and by controlling and designing the mix of technologies we release in our environments. But such an ecology of media, of culture, necessitates extensive training in the arts, and widespread training of formal awareness has ever been at odds with the demands of "practical" necessity. Perhaps it is time for the roles of artist and bureaucrat/entrepreneur to reverse positions. Our New World of chaos and complexity is too volatile, too precarious, too important to be left in the hands of the merely practical administrator.

---

170 Marshall McLuhan, opening of the last chapter of *Through the Vanishing Point: Space in Poetry and Painting*, "The Emperor's New Clothes" (New York: Harper & Row, 1968).

Appendix One

In the early 1970s, we discovered that there were invariably four general groups of effects of any new technology. And, evidently, only these four appeared in every case. We called them Laws of Media and phrased them as questions:

- What does the new thing enlarge or enhance or amplify?
- What does it retrieve or bring back in a new way?
- What, when it is pressed to an extreme, is the area of reversal?
- What does it sideline or make superfluous or "obsolete"?

Not only did these four appear in the case of technologies like radio and print and xerox, but also they applied to every human artefact of whatever kind, including clothing, styles in art, literature, music, philosophical systems, and even laws of physics and chemistry, or civil laws or parts of speech. The everyday refrigerator, for example, enhances/amplifies the availability of a wider range of foods than was possible previously, while pushing aside the older icebox. It also reduces the need for dried food and for preserving food or extending its life by means of salting and spicing. Simultaneously, the refrigerator retrieves considerable leisure for the cook as well as the provider. One of the reversals begins with the wider range of available foods and results in homogeneity of flavour and texture.

The four processes occur simultaneously with the appearance of the thing: all four are in operation from the first moment of the new item, although one or another may not appear for a while. Second, the four resonate together in a set of analogies, A is to B as C is to D.

This analogical pattern is the same structure as presented by every word in every human language that is or ever was, the structure of all metaphor. These four give the *logos*, the pattern of forces of their subject. They are an analytic of the formal cause of the item.

To help make the patterns more visible, we wrote the four "laws" at the corners of an imaginary square. The corners are identified by initials: E for enhance; R, retrieve; O, obsolesce; F, flip (reversal). (So, E is to F as R is to O, and so on.)

Here is the tetrad of laws for formal cause:

Formal Cause

Ground/figure
Interaction
The Name

Stasis
Numbness

Enhance **Flip**

Retrieve **Obsolesce**

Simultaneous,
Diachronic

Sequential,
Configurational

Appendix Two

Communication Arts in the Ancient World

All human wisdom is manifest in words, and words come in three forms: silent, written, spoken. The *logos* is therefore *the* medium—of communication as well as of the cultural bond. But under the influence of alphabetic writing, the transforming *logos* of the pre-Socratics morphed into new elements that correspond to the three verbal modes of wisdom.

The silent word is that of Dialectic, the *logos hendiathetos*. It is the word in the mind, before speech. It is the skill of thinking in words. So dialectic places its emphasis on mental processes, on logic and philosophy, and thinking aright (2 polarities; 3 parts of syllogisms).

The written word is that of Grammar, the *logos spermatikos*—the *logos* as the seeds embedded in things, the seeds from which things grow and derive their essential nature. Consequently, Grammar places its emphasis on etymology and interpretation of both the written book and the Book of Nature. Grammar bridged the arts (4 levels) and sciences (4 causes). The grammarian regarded all of Nature and every written text as his province.

The spoken word is that of Rhetoric, the *logos prophorikos*. So Rhetoric emphasizes transformation, of audience, and decorum (and all 5 divisions).

Acknowledgements

"The Relation of Environment to Anti-Environment" appeared first in the *University of Windsor Review*, Vol. 11, No. 1, Fall, 1966 (Windsor, Ontario), pp. 1-10. It was subsequently reprinted in Floyd Matson and Ashley Montagu, eds., *The Human Dialogue* (New York: Macmillan, 1967), pp. 1-10.

"*The Argument: Causality in the Electric World,*" by Marshall McLuhan and Barrington Nevitt, appeared in *Technology and Culture*, Vol. 14, #1 (University of Chicago Press, January, 1973), pp. 1-18. The response by Fr. Joseph Owens followed, on pp. 19-21, and that by Dr. Frederick Wilhelmsen on pp. 22-27.

"Formal Causality in Chesterton," by Marshall McLuhan appeared in *The Chesterton Review*, Spring/ Summer, 1976, Vol. II, No. 2, pp. 253-259.

"On Formal Cause," by Eric McLuhan first appeared in *Explorations in Media Ecology*, Vol. IV, Nos. 3/4, 2005, pp. 181-209.

Acknowledgements

I would like to thank Dr. Alexandra Wilhelmsen executrix the Estate of Frederick D. Wilhelmsen (d. 1996), for permission to reprint his essay. And I am grateful also to Richard Nevitt, executor of the Estate of Barrington Nevitt, for granting permission to use his contribution. Thanks, too, to Michael McLuhan, executor of our father's Estate. Particular recognition is also due to Lance Strate for his endless efforts, as editor of the journal, *Explorations in Media Ecology*, to ensure accuracy and readability in a thorny mixture of Greek and Latin and English. And at last I can recognize the unsung labours of Dr. Phil Rose for his generous work on the Greek passages in the essay on Formal Cause which were frequently scrambled into gibberish by unfeeling and insensitive computer programs.

—Eric McLuhan

Bibliography

Adler, Mortimer, ed. *The Great Ideas: I.* Volume Two of *Great Books of the Western World*, ed. R. M. Hutchins. Chicago: University of Chicago Press/Encyclopædia Britannica, 1952.

Aristotle. *De Anima.* Ed. Sir David Ross. Oxford: Clarendon Press, 1961.

Aristotle. *Generation of Animals.* Trans. A. L. Peck. Cambridge, MA: Harvard University Press/London: William Heinemann Ltd., 1963.

Aristotle. *On the Soul, Parva Naturalia, On Breath.* Trans. W. S. Hett Cambridge. MA: Harvard University Press/London: W. Heinemann, 1957.

Aristotle. *Parts of Animals.* London: William Heinemann/Cambridge, MA: Harvard University Press, Loeb Classical Library, 1937.

Aristotle. *The Physics.* Trans. Philip A. Wicksteed and Francis M. Cornford. In two volumes. Vol. I: 127. Loeb Cambridge, MA: Harvard University Press/London: W. Heinemann, 1980.

Aristotle. *Posterior Analytics.* Trans., Hugh Tredennick; bound with *Topica*, trans., E. S. Forster. London: William Heinemann/Cambridge, MA: Harvard University Press, Loeb Classical Library, 1960

Balazs, Etienne. *Chinese Civilization and Bureaucracy: Variations on a Theme.* New Haven, CT: Yale University Press, 1964.

Bateson, Gregory. *Steps to an Ecology of Mind: Collected Essays in Anthropology, Psychiatry, Evolution, and Epistemology.* Chicago: University Of Chicago Press, 1972.

Bret, Jane, and Frederick D. Wilhelmsen. *Telepolitics: The Politics of Neuronic Man.* Montreal and New York: Tundra Books, 1972.

Buber, Martin. *I and Thou.* Trans. Ronald Gregor Smith. New York: Macmillan, 1958.

Bunge, Mario. *Causality: The Place of the Causal Principle in Modern Science.* Cambridge: Harvard University Press, 1959.

Capek, Milic. *The Philosophical Impact of Contemporary Physics.* New York: Van Nostrand, 1961.

Chargaff, Erwin. "Preface to a Grammar of Biology." *Science* 172.3984 (1971): 637-642.

Chesterton, G. K. *Dickens.* London: Methuen, 1906.

Chesterton, G. K. *Tremendous Trifles.* New York: Dodd, Mead, 1909.

Chesterton, G. K. "The Queer Feet." *The Father Brown Stories.* London: Cassell, 1966.

Conrad, Joseph. "Preface" to *The Nigger of the 'Narcissus'.* London: Gresham Publishing Company, 1925.

Drucker, Peter F. *Managing for Results: Economic Tasks and Risk-Taking Decisions.* New York: Harper & Row, 1964.

Easterbrook W. T., and Hugh G. J. Aitken, *Canadian Economic History.* Toronto: Macmillan, 1956.

Eliot, T. S. *On Poetry and Poets.* New York: Noonday Press/Farrar, Straus & Cudahy, 1943.

Eliot, T. S. "Tradition and the Individual Talent." *The Sacred Wood: Essays on Poetry and Criticism* London: Methuen, 1920.

Ellul, Jacques. *Propaganda: The Formation of Men's Attitudes.* Trans. Konrad Kellen and Jean Lerner. New York: Knopf, 1965.

Engels Friedrich, and C. P. Dutt. *Dialectics of Nature.* Trans. J. B. S. Haldane. New York: International Publishers, 1940.

Frye, Northrop. *Anatomy of Criticism—Four Essays.* Princeton, NJ: Princeton University Press, 1957.

Frye, Northrop. *Fables of Identity: Studies in Poetic Mythology.* New York: Harcourt, Brace & World, Inc.

Fussell, Jr., Paul. *Poetic Meter and Poetic Form.* New York: Random House, 1965.

Giedion, Siegfried. *Mechanization Takes Command.* New York: Oxford University Press, 1948.

Gilson, Etienne. *Being and Some Philosophers.* Toronto: Pontifical Institute of Mediæval Studies, 1949, Rev., 1952.

Gilson, Etienne. *From Aristotle to Darwin and Back Again: A Journey in Final Causality, Species, and Evolution.* Notre Dame, Indiana: University of Notre Dame Press, 1984.

Goerres, Ida Friederike. *The Hidden Face: A Study of St. Therese of Lisieux.* New York: Pantheon, 1959.

Gombrich, E. H. *Art and Illusion: A Study in the Psychology of Pictorial Representation.* New York: Pantheon Books, 1965.

Gould, Glenn. "An Argument for Music in the Electronic Age." *Varsity Graduate* 11:3 (1964): 118-120.

Hall, Edward T. *The Silent Language.* Garden City, NY: Doubleday, 1959.

Havelock, Eric A. *Preface to Plato.* Cambridge, MA: The Belknap Press of Harvard University Press, 1963.

Havelock, Eric A. *Prologue to Greek Literacy.* Cincinnati: University of Cincinnati, 1971.

Havelock, Eric A. *The Muse Learns to Write: Reflections on Orality and Literacy from Antiquity to the Present.* New Haven and London: Yale University Press, 1986.

Hawking, Stephen. *Black Holes and Baby Universes and Other Essays.* New York, London, Toronto, Sydney, Auckland: Bantam Books, 1993.

Heidegger, Martin. *The Question Concerning Technology and Other Essays.* Trans. William Levitt. New York: Harper Colophon Books, 1977.

Hildebrand, Adolf. *The Problem of Form in Painting and Sculpture*, 2nd ed., Trans. and rev. Max Meyer and Robert Morris Ogden. New York: G. E. Stechert & Co., 1932.

Hockney, David. *Secret Knowledge: Discovering the Lost Techniques of the Old Masters.* London: Thames and Hudson, 2001.

Illich, Ivan. *In the Vineyard of the Text: A Commentary to Hugh of St. Victor's* Didascalion. Chicago and London: University of Chicago Press, 1993.

Innis, Harold A. *The Bias of Communication.* Toronto: University of Toronto Press, 1964.

Isaacs, J. *The Background of Modern Poetry.* New York: Dutton, 1952.

Jacobs, Jane. *The Economy of Cities.* New York: Random House, 1969.

Johnson, Steven. *Emergence: The Connected Lives of Ants, Brains, Cities, and Software.* New York: Scribner, 2001.

Joyce, James. *Finnegans Wake* New York: Viking, 1939.

Koestler, Arthur. *The Act of Creation.* New York: Macmillan, 1964.

Korzybski, Alfred. *Science and Sanity: An Introduction to Non-Aristotelian Systems and General Semantics,* 5th ed. Englewood, NJ: Institute of General Semantics, 1994.

Kuhn, Thomas S. *The Structure of Scientific Revolutions.* Chicago: University of Chicago Press, 1962.

Lain-Entralgo, Pedro. *Therapy of the Word in Classical Antiquity.* Ed. and trans. L. J. Rather and J. M. Sharp. New Haven and London: Yale University Press, 1970.

Leclerq, Jean. *The Love of Learning and the Desire for God.* New York: Fordham University Press, 1982.

Long, Marcus. *The Spirit of Philosophy.* Toronto: University of Toronto Press, 1953.

Lund, Nils Wilhelm. *Chiasmus in the New Testament: A Study in Formgeschichte.* Chapel Hill: University of North Carolina Press, 1942.

Lusseyran, Jacques. *And There Was Light.* Boston: Little, Brown, 1963.

Malraux, André. *The Museum Without Walls.* Trans. Stuart Gilbert. London : A. Zwemmer, 1949.

Mandelbrot, Benoit. *The Fractal Geometry of Nature.* San Francisco, CA: W. H. Freeman, 1983.

Maturana, Humberto R., and Francisco J. Varela, *Autopoiesis and Cognition: The Realization of the Living.* Boston: D. Reidel, 1980.

McLuhan, Eric. *The Role of Thunder in* Finnegans Wake. Toronto: University of Toronto Press, 1997.

McLuhan, Eric. "Francis Bacon's Theory of Communication." *Going for Baroque: Cultural Transformations 1550-1650.* Ed. Francesco Guardiani. Brooklyn, NY: Legas, 1999.

McLuhan, Marshall. *The Mechanical Bride: Folklore of Industrial Man* New York: Vanguard Press, 1951.

McLuhan, Marshall. *The Gutenberg Galaxy: The Making of Typographic Man.* Toronto: University of Toronto Press, 1962.

McLuhan, Marshall. *Understanding Media: The Extensions of Man.* New York: McGraw-Hill, 1964.

McLuhan, Marshall. "Education in the Electronic Age." *The Best of Times/The Worst of Times: Contemporary Issues in Canadian Education.* Eds. H. A. Stevenson, R. M. Stamp, and J. D. Wilson. Toronto and Montreal: Holt, Rinehart and Winston of Canada Limited, 1972. 530-531.

McLuhan, Marshall. "Laws of Media." *ETC: A Review of General Semantics* 34:2 (1977): 173-179.

McLuhan, Marshall. *Letters of Marshall McLuhan.* Eds. Matie Molinaro, Corrine McLuhan, and William Toye. Toronto: Oxford University Press, 1987.

McLuhan, Marshall. *The Medium and the Light.* Eds. Eric McLuhan and Jacek Szlarek. Toronto: Stoddart, 1999.

McLuhan, Marshall. *The Classical Trivium: The Place of Thomas Nashe in the Learning of his Time.* Corte Madera, CA: Gingko Press, 2006.

McLuhan, Marshall, and Quentin Fiore. *The Medium is the Massage: An Inventory of Effects* New York: Bantam Books, 1967.

McLuhan, Marshall, and Quentin Fiore. *War and Peace in the Global Village: An Inventory of Some of the Current Spastic Situations that Could be Eliminated by More Feedforward.* New York: Bantam Books, 1968.

McLuhan Marshall, and Eric McLuhan. *Laws of Media: The New Science.* Toronto: University of Toronto Press, 1988.

McLuhan, Marshall, and Barrington Nevitt. *Take Today: The Executive as Dropout.* New York: Harcourt Brace Jovanovich, 1972.

McLuhan Marshall, and Harley Parker. *Through the Vanishing Point: Space in Poetry and Painting.* New York: Harper and Row, 1968.

McLuhan Marshall, and Harley Parker. *Counterblast.* New York: Harcourt Brace & World, 1969.

McLuhan Marshall, and Wilfred Watson. *From Cliché to Archetype.* New York: Viking Press, 1970.

Meyer, Nicholas. *The Seven-Per-Cent Solution: Being a Reprint from the Reminiscences of John H. Watson, M.D., as edited by Nicholas Meyer.* New York: Ballantine Books, 1974, 1975.

Mill, John Stuart. *A System of Logic.* 9th ed. London: Longmans, Green, Reader, and Dyer, 1875.

Miller Arthur, "1949: The Year It Came Apart." *New York Magazine* 30 Dec. 1974.

Newman, John Henry Cardinal. *An Essay on the Development of Christian Doctrine.* New York: Doubleday, 1960.

Owens, Fr. Joseph. *An Interpretation of Existence.* Milwaukee: Bruce Publishing, 1968.

Pauling, Linus. *The Nature of the Chemical Bond and the Structures of Molecules and Crystals: An Introduction to Modern Chemistry.* 3rd ed. Ithaca, NY: Cornell University Press, 1960,

Polanyi, Michael. *The Tacit Dimension.* Garden City, NY, 1967.

Popper, Karl R. *The Logic of Scientific Discovery.* New York: Basic Books, 1959.

Pound, Ezra. *ABC of Reading.* New York: J. Laughlin, New Directions Paperback No. 89, 1960.

Pound, Ezra. "The Serious Artist." *Literary Essays of Ezra Pound,* Ed. T. S. Eliot. New York: New Directions, 1968.

Prigogine, Ilya, and Isabelle Stengers, *Order Out of Chaos: Man's New Dialogue with Nature.* London: Flamingo, 1984.

Rosenthal, Raymond, ed. *McLuhan: Pro and Con.* New York: Funk & Wagnalls, 1968.

Schon, Donald Alan. *Displacement of Concepts.* London: Tavistock Publications, 1963.

Steiner, George. *After Babel.* London, New York, Toronto: Oxford University Press, 1975.

Strate, Lance. *Echoes and Reflections: On Media Ecology as a Field of Study.* Cresskill, NJ: Hampton Press, 2006.

Strate, Lance and Edward Wachtel, eds. *The Legacy of McLuhan.* Cresskill, NJ: Hampton Press, 2005.

Volk, Tyler. *Metapatterns: Across Space, Time, and Mind.* New York: Columbia University Press, 1995.

Wilhelmsen, Frederick D. “Reasoning and Computers.” *Thought* 45:179 (1970): 169-179.

Wilhelmsen, Frederick D. *The Paradoxical Structure of Existence.* Irving, TX: University of Dallas Press, 1970.

Index

About the Authors

Marshall McLuhan (1911 - 1980) attended the University of Manitoba and there earned a B.A. and M.A. in English (1934). He then attended Cambridge University and received the B.A., M.A., and Ph.D. in English (1944).

He taught at the University of Wisconsin, the University of St. Louis, Assumption University (Windsor, 1944) and St. Michael's College (Toronto, 1946-1980), where he headed the interdisciplinary Centre for Culture and Technology. Besides many hundreds of articles in a broad variety of magazines and journals, he has written over twenty books. These include *The Mechanical Bride: The Folklore of Industrial Man*; *Alfred Lord Tennyson: Selected Poetry*; *The Gutenberg Galaxy: The Making of Typographic Man*; *Understanding Media: The Extensions of Man*; *The Classical Trivium: The Place of Thomas Nashe in the Learning of his Time*; *Voices of Literature* (three volumes; with Richard Schoeck); *Verbi-Voco-Visual Explorations*; *The Medium is the Massage*; *War and Peace in the Global Village*; *Through the Vanishing Point: Space in Poetry and Painting* (with Harley Parker); *The Interior Landscape: The Literary Criticism of Marshall McLuhan, 1943-1962*; *Counterblast* (designed by Harley Parker); *Mutations 1990*; *Culture is Our Business*; *From Cliché to Archetype* (with Wilfred Watson); *Take Today: The Executive as Drop Out* (with Barry Nevitt); *City as Classroom: Understanding Language and Media* (with Kathryn Hutchon and Eric

McLuhan); *D'oeil a Oreille, Autre homme autre chretien a l'age electronique* (with Pierre Babin).

Posthumous publications include the following: *Letters of Marshall McLuhan*; *Laws of Media: The New Science* (with Eric McLuhan); *The Global Village: Transformations in World Life and Media in the 21st Century* (with Bruce Powers); *Marshall McLuhan: The Man and His Message*; *Essential McLuhan*; *Forward Through the Rear View Mirror: Reflections on and by Marshall McLuhan*; *The Medium and the Light: Reflections on Religion and Media*; *The Book of Probes*; *Understanding Me: Lectures and Interviews*; *McLuhan Unbound*; *Theories of Communication* (with Eric McLuhan); and the present volume, *Media and Formal Cause* (with Eric McLuhan).

Marshall McLuhan is recognized as the inventor of the field of media study. In *Laws of Media*, he showed the seamless relation between literary criticism and understanding new media and artifacts, and he demonstrated that the new tools for media study had dissolved the long-held division between the arts and the sciences. This book concerns one of the principal such tools.

Eric McLuhan received his B. Sc. in Communication from Wisconsin State University in 1972. He got the M. A. and Ph. D. in English Literature from the University of Dallas in 1980 and 1982. An internationally-known lecturer on communication and media, he has over forty years' teaching experience in subjects ranging from high-speed reading techniques to English literature, media, and communication theory, and has taught at many colleges and universities in both the United States and Canada.

He has published articles in magazines and professional journals since 1964 on media, perception, and literature, and assisted Marshall McLuhan with the research and writing of *The Medium is the Massage, War and Peace in the Global Village, Culture is Our Business, From Cliché to Archetype,* and *Take Today: The Executive as Drop-Out.* He is co-author: with Marshall McLuhan and Kathryn Hutchon, of *City as Classroom* (Irwin, 1977); with Marshall McLuhan, of *Laws of Media: The New Science* (University of Toronto Press, 1988); and with Wayne Constantineau, of *The Human Equation* (Toronto: BPS Books, 2010).

Eric McLuhan is the author of *The Role of Thunder in* Finnegans Wake (University of Toronto Press, 1997); *Electric Language: Understanding the Present* (Stoddart, 1998); and *Theories of Communication* (New York: Peter Lang, 2010). He is the co-editor of: *Essential McLuhan* (Stoddart, 1995), and *Who Was Marshall McLuhan?* (1994; Stoddart, 1995), and the editor of: *The Medium and the Light* (Stoddart, 1999); the academic journal, *McLuhan Studies*; and editor, for Gingko Press, of: *Understanding Media, Critical Edition* (2003); *McLuhan Unbound* (2004); and *The Book of Probes* (2004), and was consulting editor for Voyager/Southam's "McLuhan Project," which produced *Understanding McLuhan* (1997), a CD on Marshall McLuhan and his work.

NeoPoiesis
a new way of making

in ancient Greece, poiesis referred to the process of making
creation – production – organization – formation – causation
a process that can be physical and spiritual
biological and intellectual
artistic and technological
material and teleological
efficient and formal
a means of modifying the environment
and a method of organizing the self
the making of art and music and poetry
the fashioning of memory and history and philosophy
the construction of perception and expression and reality

NeoPoiesis Press
reflecting the creative drive and spirit
of the new electronic media environment

Breinigsville, PA USA
21 February 2011
256011BV00004B/7/P

9 780983 274704